SQUIRRELS

SQUIRRELS

A Wildlife Handbook

Kim Long

SCIENTIFIC ADVISOR
Dr. Vagn Flyger
Professor Emeritus, University of Maryland

Johnson Books: Boulder

Published in the United States by Johnson Books, a Division of Johnson Publishing Company, 1880 South 57th Court, Boulder, Colorado 80301.

9   8   7   6   5   4

All illustrations by the author except where otherwise indicated.

Library of Congress Cataloging-in-Publication Data
Long, Kim.
    Squirrels : a wildlife handbook / Kim Long. —1 ed.
        p.   cm.
    Includes bibliographical references (p.   ) and index.
    ISBN 1-55566-152-1 (alk. paper)
    1. Squirrels—Handbooks, manuals, etc.   I. Title.
QL737.R68L66   1995
599.32'32—dc20   95-43163
                                                                            CIP

Printed in the United States by
Johnson Printing
1880 South 57th Court
Boulder, Colorado 80301

 Printed on recycled paper with soy ink

CONTENTS

Acknowledgments viii

Introduction ix

Tales of Yore 1

Names 20

Squirrel Species 23

    Comparing Squirrel Sizes 24

    Squirrel Measurements 25

    Eastern Gray Squirrel 26

    Western Gray Squirrel 30

    Fox Squirrel 34

    Red Squirrel 38

    Douglas Squirrel 42

    Southern Flying Squirrel 46

    Northern Flying Squirrel 50

    Abert's Squirrel 54

    Arizona Gray Squirrel 58

Taxonomy 59

Squirrel Anatomy

    Teeth 71

    Eyes 72

    Ears 72

    Sense of Smell 73

    Fur 75

Feet 78

Tail 79

Diet 81

Nut Menu 82

Nut Facts 83

Favorite Foods 87

Food Trees 89

Pine Cone Menu 90

Animal Food Sources 91

Fungi Menu 93

Plant Food Sources 94

The Natural History of Pine Cones 98

The Natural History of Acorns 102

Acorn Menu 103

Seasonal Diet 105

Hoarding 106

Squirrels in Motion 113

Flying Squirrels 116

Nests 118

Nest Varieties 120

Territory 122

Home Turf 123

Reproduction 125

Squirrel Signs 130

Food Debris 130

Tracks 131

Scat 132

Bark Marks 132

Squirrel Sounds 133

Migration 134

The Squirrel Menace 137

Bird Feeders: Squirrel Defense 140

Feeding Squirrels 141

Squirrel Houses 147

Squirrel Removal 149

Endangered Squirrels 151

Profile of a Squirrel 153

Parasites 154

Causes of Death 157

Predators 158

More Squirrel Predators 160

Profile of a Predator 163

Edible Squirrels 164

Resources 167

Online Resources 169

Squirrel Aid 170

Squirrel Products 171

Bibliography 173

Index 178

ACKNOWLEDGMENTS

Vagn Flyger: master of squirrel information
Denver Public Library
Western History Collection, Denver Public Library
Auraria Library, Metropolitan State College
Norlin Library, University of Colorado
Kathleen Cain, Front Range Community College
Roseanne Humprey, Zoology Department, University of Colorado
Dr. Randall Lockwood, Humane Society of the U.S.
Christopher Richard, Oakland Museum
Bill Alther, Denver Museum of Natural History
Field Museum of Natural History, Chicago
Janeen Devine, Field Museum Library
Stage House II
Virginia Auer, Michael Auer: nurturers of squirrels
Pat Wagner, Leif Smith
Greg McNamee
The Bloomsbury Review
Larry Conner, Arapahoe Coin & Stamp Company
Wild Birds Unlimited
Wild Bird Center

 A special thanks to the hard-working dermestid beetles (aka *carpet beetles*) of the Denver Museum of Natural History for their help in preparing a specimen for use in illustration. In their natural habitat these insects and their larvae eat decaying animals, part of the natural recycling system of nature.

INTRODUCTION

Pity the poor tree squirrel. Throughout history, it has rarely been the object of much attention. Ignored both as a heroic beast and as despicable vermin, the squirrel has inspired few myths, poems, or art.

What can be the reason? Are their industrious habits too insignificant to rate notice? Are they shrugged off as a second-rate nuisance, raiders of gardens and petty thieves of bird food? In reality, squirrels are likely to be the most common wildlife that the average city-dweller comes close to, barring pigeons. Perhaps because they are so common, they are overlooked. Throughout history, this has been a continuing theme, with the common squirrel losing out as an animal symbol, largely left out of myths, religions, folk tales, popular songs — not to mention books — in favor of more glamorous beasts, the tigers, eagles, and whales of the world. Whatever the reason, there is much to ponder about the family of squirrels, from their unique tails to their evolutionary development in tune with trees such as the oak and pine.

Here you will find facts, myths, mysteries, interactions with human cultures, graphics, and newly emerging information uncovered by ongoing research. For closet squirrel lovers and urban wildlife fans as well as those already enamored of this widespread creature, this is one small step in making up for past omissions.

TALES OF YORE

"The gray squirrel, like the deer, skunk, raccoon, red fox, and cottontail rabbit, nonetheless prospers at the edges of civilizations, and where not unduly persecuted these species have increased." — Peter Matthiessen

The tree squirrel, a member of the rodent order, dwells on most continents and in most countries. The species native to the American continent were a familiar part of the environmental heritage of native Americans. Tribes from coast to coast used the squirrel for food and clothing material and images of the squirrel appear in some tribal culture as talismans, folklore, and mythology. In early Europe, too, the squirrel played a role in the mythology of different groups.

Old Ireland, the home of Gaelic tradition, was covered with forests, most of which disappeared in the Middle Ages as the population expanded and the need for lumber and firewood increased. Another major factor in the decline of these woodlands was the development of the iron industry; smelting iron required huge quantities of charcoal, made from the available supply of hardwoods. With the shrinking of the woodlands, mammals dependent on this ecosystem declined in numbers and were vanquished to parks and the remaining small stands of trees.

In the United States, most squirrel populations have abundant room to maintain their genetic diversity and thrive as species. This is despite the severe reduction in size of the forest ecosystem in the four hundred plus years since European colonization began. Primarily because of agricultural demand, traditional forests have been converted to crops and pastureland. In many areas, the remaining trees are limited to small stands that are insufficient to supply a breeding colony

THE NORTH AMERICAN TREE SQUIRREL

a.k.a. *chickaree, fairydiddle, silvertail, graytail, cat squirrel, grayback, bannertail, piney sprite, puck-o'-the-pines, red robber, rusty squirrel, black squirrel, silver-tail, white-tail, yellow piney, yellow-belly, egg robber, tree rat*

of squirrels with food and even worse for the squirrels, the stands are widely separated, creating islands of woods isolated by large tracts of open farmland. With few safe avenues of travel, squirrels and other native forest-dwelling animals are not able to maintain the natural population cycles they have been accustomed to. On the other hand, the crops with which the forests have been replaced have often provided a new and beneficial source of food for native squirrels, although farmers may disagree that this is necessarily a good thing. Corn especially has been a boon for squirrels. Gray and fox squirrels often feast on this agricultural staple and can cause considerable losses when their numbers are high.

Despite the expanses of farmland and urban sprawl, however, some species of squirrels have adapted well to new habitats. The gray squirrel in particular seems to be a big winner in the urbanization of the countryside. Gray squirrels are the primary squirrel found in cities, the ones most likely to thrive in this new non-natural habitat, characterized by a mix of native and non-native plants, flower and vegetable gardens, garbage, bird feeders, and free handouts.

Some biologists, in fact, believe the urban habitat is more suited to the lifestyle of the gray squirrel than its original environment.

The animal we know as the tree squirrel was as familiar in ancient times as today. The word squirrel, in fact, comes from the Greek syllables *skia* meaning "shadow," and *oura*, meaning "tail." The animal with the shadow tail, however, was never referred to in ancient Greek writing; it most likely came from common usage, the dialect of everyday speech. In ancient Greece, just as in today's world, the squirrel was often overlooked.

In modern science, Latin is the language used to formerly label life forms, both plants and animals. Squirrels are referred to as *sciurus*, a word borrowed from the Greek.

"We also, during this day's journey, first noticed the common red barking squirrel, which, invited from its nest, by the beauty of the weather during the afternoon, has been frequently observed playing among the branches of the black walnut, and other favourite trees. This sprightly little animal is equally entitled to our admiration from the beauty of its form and the agility of its movements; and there is no person who has visited an American forest during the summer season, either as a sportsman or an admirer of nature, who is not ready to acknowledge how much this pretty and playful little quadruped contributes to enliven and beautify the scene."

— Henry R. Schoolcraft
Narrative Journal of Travels Through the Northwestern Regions of the United States Extending from Detroit Through the Great Chain of American Lakes to the Sources of the Mississippi River in the Year 1820

Other cultures in North America and around the world have their own words to describe tree squirrels.

Choctaw: fani okchako ("blue squirrel")
Chinook: ap-poe-poe
Natick: mishe-anéqus ("big chipmunk")
Ojibwa: kitchi-adjidamo ("big squirrel")
Cherokee: salà' li
Chippewa: kleé-ay
French: écureuil
German: eichhörnchen, eichkatze (literally, "oak-tree cat")
Hopi: scha-ghern-uh
Italian: scoiattolo
Natick: mishannek
Oglala Sioux: zee-cha
Spanish: ardilla
Swedish: ekorr
Danish: egern
Yankton Sioux: kee-hah-chah
Yiddish: veverke
Bengali: katbirali ("female cat in a tree")
Mongolian: kherem (no translation)
Chinese: sungshü (pine rat)
Japanese: mezumi (rat)
       kinezumi
       risu

These kanji are traditional words used to mean *squirrel* in Japanese (*risu* or *kinezumi*).

Squirrels have achieved a minor place of distinction in heraldry, the system of traditional designs and symbols used to denote family identity in England and Europe. The image of the squirrel stands for retirement or retreat to the forest. Families which originally had squirrels in their crests include Baldwin, Lee, Samuels, and Chambers.

ecause squirrels are common to cultures throughout most of the world, legends and myths about them are also found in many societies. Mentions of squirrels being transformed into other animals, stealing from other animals, and even marrying humans are found in India, Iceland, Finland, France, Indonesia, Alaska, and Russia. The lowly squirrel, however, has no exalted status as an animal figure in mythic literature. Constellations have been named after swans, rabbits, and lions; gods and other deities are often transformed from monkeys, elephants, and eagles; turtles, deer, and whales are routinely associated with creation myths. But

A unique illustration of a tree squirrel from an unknown 19th century engraver.

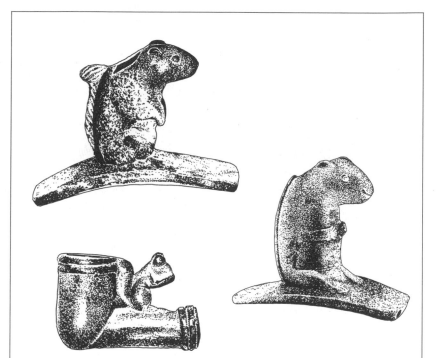

Squirrel effigy tobacco pipes from a collection in the Ohio State Museum. Size: each is about 3.5 x 2.5 inches (90 mm x 60 mm). These pipes were found in the Tremper Mound, situated near the present city of Portsmouth, Ohio. The mound was constructed by a tribe of the Hopewell culture, a pre-Columbian culture that thrived from approximately 500 B.C. to about 500 A.D. These pipes are made of pipestone (catlinite), a soft mineralized clay found in southwestern Minnesota and widely traded throughout the midwestern and eastern native American populations. Squirrels were a common part of the diet of the mound cultures, as evidenced by the number of squirrel bones found in excavations of these sites.

squirrels have gotten the short stick for glory in most cultures, both past and present.

Typical of the status of the squirrel in cultural history is its portrayal in Norse mythology. Ratatosk is a squirrel who runs up and down the Yggdrasil (the sacred tree), busy stirring up trouble between the eagle at the top and the serpent at the bottom. Ratatosk also was a messenger for Odin, bringing to him reports from the world of humans.

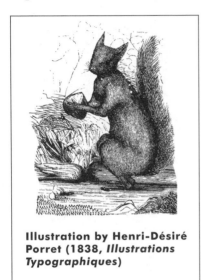

Illustration by Henri-Désiré Porret (1838, *Illustrations Typographiques*)

In Asia, the image of the squirrel was common as a decorative motif in several countries. In China, the squirrel was often represented with the grapevine because both the grapevine and the squirrel were capable of creeping over all available surfaces. In the ancient Ainu culture of Japan, squirrels were referred to in literature as the cast-off sandals of the goddess Aioina. The flesh of the squirrel was called *At kamui* (the Divine Prolific One) and was believed to be a cure for infertility. Squirrel meat was also sought after by those needing new teeth because the gnawing activity of this animal was thought to imbue it with special power.

In western religion there is also the presence of the squirrel. Early Christian art occasionally included images of squirrels, sometimes in paintings of Saint Jerome. Such Christian applications often used the image of the squirrel to emphasize an aphorism or moral. In a picture of a squirrel enduring a rainstorm under the protection of its tail, an inscription reads:

Illustration by Gertrude S. Kinder for *The Red Indian Fairy Book* by Frances Jenkins Olcott. Republished in 1923 in *The Child's Treasury* (Foundation Desk Company, Chicago).

"Durabo, et quondam res expectabo secunda
Quamvis nunc male sit, non male semper erit."
(*I shall endure and expect once again more favorable things*
However bad it is now, it won't be bad forever)

In an illustrated manuscript from 1595, a picture of a squirrel is shown, using its tail to sail across a river. The inscription reads:
"Vincit solertia vires"
(*Inventiveness vanquishes might*)

Some native American tribes included the squirrel as part of their traditional folklore. A Passamaquoddy (one of the Algonquin tribes) legend relates that the squirrel, *miko*, was originally larger than the bear, but *Glooskap*, the creator, used his hands to "smooth" him down to his current size. The squirrel then became like a pet dog to Glooskap. Whenever

Glooskap needed help, miko expanded to his previous size
and dispatched Glooskap's enemies.

The Ojibwa tribe provided the basis of the well-known
stories popularized by "The Song of Hiawatha," written by
Henry W. Longfellow in 1855. These stories were based on a
collection of Ojibwa stories originally collected by Henry
Rowe Schoolcraft.

> "And the squirrel, Adjidaumo,
> Frisked and chatted very gayly,
> Toiled and tugged with Hiawatha
> Till the labor was completed.
> Then said Hiawatha to him,
> 'O my little friend, the squirrel,
> Bravely have you toiled to help me;
> Take the thanks of Hiawatha,
> And the name which now he gives you;
> Far hereafter and forever
> Boys shall call you Adjidaumo,
> Tail-in-air the boys shall call you!'"

One of the Navajo creation myths tells of animal people
who thrived in the world below before there was a sun or a
moon. The pine squirrel people were known as *Klozêslskái.*

The squirrel also appears as a potent symbol for the Navajo
deity *Hascheltî,* Talking God. Sacred corn meal, an important
part of many Navajo rituals, is carried by this god in a pouch
made from a pine squirrel.

In the late 1700s, a European explorer observed the Chippewa Indians in Canada attempting to improve their luck
when fishing by using charms made of bits of beaver tail,
otter teeth, muskrat intestines, human hair, and squirrel testicles.

The Kwakiutl tribe of the Vancouver region also placed
importance on the power of the squirrel. In order to improve

the future hunting and fighting prowess of their sons, they fed their male infants pieces of squirrel hearts to pass on the squirrels' ability to dash quickly from one place to another.

Among the Cherokee, the meat of the squirrel was traditionally tabu for those with rheumatism. This was because the squirrel ate while hunched over. Squirrels in general, however, were seen as positive images by Indian cultures because they provided meat and fur.

Effigies of the squirrel were used in some decorative applications, including carved into tobacco pipes, and squirrel fur was a decorative part of some tribal costumes. The Shasta tribe used brushes made from the tail hair of squirrels as sponges, soaking up berry juice from bowls and then sucking the brushes dry. Some tribes also used squirrel fur as towels and blankets, especially for newborns.

Illustration from a spelling book from the early 1800s.

Early European Americans developed their own folklore about the native wildlife. Squirrels were often seen as talismans. A squirrel crossing your path, for instance, could bring good luck, also ensured by carrying a squirrel's tail. On the other hand, another early superstition — attributed to African Americans in southern states — attributed bad luck to the squirrel. A particularly bad sign was if a flying squirrel was found inside a house. This was thought to be an omen for the loss of a family member before the end of the month. A variation on this omen held that this act pretold the destruction of the house.

A traditional European superstition held that sudden chills running up and down your spine meant that someone was walking or standing on your future grave. The folk variation on this theme in early America blamed this act on a squirrel or rabbit.

Squirrels could also be used for black magic. One folk recipe among some African Americans relied on a variety of odd ingredients, including squirrel, to make a "tricken-bag" with which to bring disease or bad luck to an enemy. The recipe called for "the wing of a jaybird, the jaw of a squirrel ... the fang of a rattlesnake ... the blood of a pig-eating sow" and other materials, wrapped in the skin of a cat.

Illustration by V.H. Kirkbride for a poem by Mary F. Butts (*The Child's Treasury*, 1923)

Squirrel activity could also be linked to omens. A folk belief attributed to Hungary held that a squirrel falling from a tree was bad luck. A German superstition linked bad luck to disturbing a squirrel while it was gathering nuts.

An old remedy for babies cutting their first teeth: rub their gums with squirrel brains. Squirrel fat was also supposedly a cure for earache and toothache.

The two attributes of the squirrel most often held up for cultural esteem are its teeth and its tail. Squirrels' tails could be carried as a good luck charm — much like rabbits' feet — and the teeth were promoted for special power. An old wive's tale regarding matrimony promoted their use in forseeing future mates. In order for an answer to be revealed in a dream, the teeth were supposed to be placed under the pillow, with the anxious lad or lass saying:

"Ninny, ninny, little squirrel
That chatters in the tree,
Tell me who my true love is to be."

BORROWED NAMES

Other flora and fauna named after the squirrel include:
squirrel cup (hepatica), squirrel grass, squirrel-tail grass, squirrel hake, squirrelfish, squirrel monkey, squirrel mouse, squirrel corn, squirrel food (death camass), squirrel frog, squirrel hawk (rough-legged hawk), squirrel mouse (dormouse), squirrel plague (tularemia), squirrel shrew, squirrel's foot fern

Most squirrel tales, however, connected its activity to the weather, and some of these folk beliefs persist in modern times. One of the most common of these holds that when squirrels begin to store nuts early in the fall, it is an omen of a long, cold winter. Squirrels growing extra heavy fur also can mean a cold winter; if they are observed burying food caches extra deep, the winter will be long. When squirrels are

"Among the necessary tasks of the local farmer, which the European immigrant at first is inclined to regard as mere sport, is that of shooting squirrels. Yes, shooting or catching squirrels is considered work here, without which no corn harvest can be expected. As soon as the seedlings appear above ground whole hordes of these little animals attack them. If they are not prevented from digging up the sprouting kernels they will surely eat them all...There are various kinds of squirrels here, but the gray species is the most numerous and the one that is a menace to cornfields. The better the walnuts develop the less the cornfields suffer. The little thieves soon learn what they have permission to do. One must creep up to cornfields in order to get within shooting distance. As soon as they see a human being approach they retreat quickly into the forest. On the other hand, they eat walnuts without the slightest fear of man."

— Gottfried Duden
Report on a Journey to the Western States of North America, 1829

SQUIRREL TRIVIA

From the Dodge City Times (April 6, 1878): "The family of Judge Beverley mourn the loss of a pet squirrel. His squirrelship was buried with great pomp and ceremony by the younger members of the family."

seen gathering or burying nuts, it is generally a sign that winter is due, but if squirrels are playing in the fall instead of being more industrious, it is a sign that the winter will be mild.

The earliest description of squirrels from the new world was in *Nouvel Atlas*, an annotated map of the Canadian region, written in 1534 by W.J. Blaeu. In 1609, Captain John Smith wrote about the flying squirrels common in the area of the Jamestown Colony in what is now the state of Virginia.

"A small beast they have they call Assapanick, but we call them flying squirrels, because spreading their legs, and so stretching the largeness of their skins, that they have beene seene to fly 30 to 40 yards."

Another early description of the flying squirrels came from Herman Moll in his book, *Compleat Geographer*, written in 1723. "The strange ones unknown to us, are the flying squirrel, so call'd because it has a fleshy substance like Wings, which it extends, and by the Help of it skips from Tree to Tree, tho' they be 20 or 30 yards distant."

Although several scientific studies about American wildlife were published in the next hundred years, it was not until the publication of *The Quadrapeds of North America*, the pioneering work of John James Audubon and the Reverend John Bachman in 1840, that organized descriptions of new

SQUIRREL TRIVIA

According to The Concord Monitor (Concord, New Hampshire) on July 19, 1934, a pet squirrel accidentally fell out of the window of a hotel in New York City. The animal fell from the sixteenth floor down an air shaft to the third floor. Hotel workers heard the squirrel land with a thump and found it, stunned and with a bloody nose, but alive. The Old Farmer's Almanac reports this as the "longest nonfatal squirrel drop in recorded history."

world tree squirrels were made widely available. In their effort, however, they frequently made errors in determining the similarities and difference of many squirrel species, often believing that various color phases of the same squirrel meant they belonged to different species. Among the distinctive species of squirrels they identified as new were the Wooly Squirrel, The Downy Squirrel, the Red-Bellied Squirrel, the Red-Tailed Squirrel, the Hare Squirrel, the Weasel-like Squirrel, and the Large Louisiana Black Squirrel.

The hunting of squirrels was an important part of the settlement of the country by native Americans and European cultures because they were a source of protein throughout the year. Hunting squirrels, however, was also important to both cultures because of the destruction squirrels could bring to agricultural crops, the major source of food for both Indians and colonists. Squirrels, along with birds, rabbits, and other small mammals, attacked corn and other grain crops and competed for natural supplies of nuts and fruits.

SQUIRREL TRIVIA

The word squirrel has also been used to describe a reckless driver or hot-rodder and a person shunned by a social clique. At one time, whiskey was referred to as squirrel. In more common usage, both psychiatrists and eccentrics have been called squirrels, and their common place of residence, the mental hospital, was referred to as a squirrel ranch.

squirrel cage: an exercise wheel or air circulator

to squirrel away: to stash or cache something

to squirrel: climbing to the top of a railroad car to manually set the brakes.

seam squirrels: body lice

From A Classical Dictionary of the Vulgar Tongue, published in 1785:

squirrel. A prostitute: because she like that animal, covers her back with her tail. Meretrix corpore corpus alit.

hunting the squirrel. An amusement practised by postboys and stage-coachmen, which consists in following a one-horse chaise, and driving it before them, passing close to it, so as to brush the wheel, and by other means terrifying any woman or person that may be in it.

Illustration by Thomas Bewick (1826)

Before the age of firearms, squirrels were often hunted with slings or arrows. Some Indian tribes employed snares for nabbing these animals. In some tribal cultures, squirrels were too small and insignificant as legitimate game for adults; hunting squirrels was considered a pastime for young boys, useful in developing hunting skills.

From the earliest days of the colonies, squirrel control regulations were common because of the threat squirrels posed to agriculture. Bounties were offered for squirrels in some cases. In the 1700s, parts of the Ohio territory required settlers to produce a certain number of squirrel heads or tails along with county taxes.

Group hunting efforts were also common. Contests were held to reduce squirrel populations through competitive shooting. In 1834 in Indiana, one such three-day contest resulted in one person shooting 900 squirrels; a week-long squirrel hunt in Ohio resulted in a reported kill of 10,000 squirrels.

Squirrels are not easy prey for hunters and have long been established as a tricky, difficult target. In colonial America, squirrel hunting skills helped develop marksmanship that was a powerful force in the defeat of the well-trained British military. Scouts for the revolutionary forces were referred to as *Squirreltails* in reference to this skill.

OFFICIAL SQUIRRELS

1987 POSTAGE STAMP FROM THE UNITED STATES

1966 POSTAGE STAMP FROM SWITZERLAND

1992 CURRENCY FROM LATVIA (OUT OF CIRCULATION)

NAMES

SOUTHERN FLYING SQUIRREL   *Glaucomys volans*
From the Greek, *glaukos* meaning grey or silver, and *mys* a variation of *mus*, meaning mouse; *volans* is from the Latin, meaning flying. Early naturalists first classified it in 1758, although it was described by the earliest settlers, including John Smith of the Virginia colony in 1624.

NORTHERN FLYING SQUIRREL   *Glaucomys sabrinus*
Sabrinus is a Latin name for river nymph, a reference to the Severn River on the west coast of Hudson Bay where the animal was originally spotted. In some localities in its range, these animals are also called "fairy diddles." First scientific reports of this animal occurred in 1788 but it was not given its current scientific name until 1801.

GRAY SQUIRREL   *Sciurus carolinensis*
Carolinensis is a Latinized word meaning of or from Carolina, the American colony where it was first observed by European observers. The first published record of this squirrel was in 1788. Audubon was one of several naturalists who originally called this the Migratory squirrel, in reference to its tendency for mass migrations.

ARIZONA GRAY SQUIRREL   *Sciurus arizonensis*
This distinct species of squirrel was named after its principal range, the state of Arizona. It was first described in 1867 and named by Elliott Coues, an army doctor and naturalist.

AMERICAN RED SQUIRREL   *Tamiasciurus hudsonicus*
From the Greek, *tamias* stands for one who stores or hoards. *Hudsonicus* is the Latinized word form indicating belonging, in this case, to Hudson Bay, where European naturalists first reported it in 1771. The original observers

called it the Hudsons Bay squirrel. In the United States, this squirrel has traditionally been called the *chickaree*, a made-up word representing the typical call of this animal. Other common names: pine squirrel, fairydiddle.

DOUGLAS SQUIRREL   *Tamiasciurus douglasii*
This West Coast animal is named after one of the earliest European naturalists who visited the region, David Douglas, who lived from 1798-1834, and also has his name on a familiar tree, the Douglas fir. Douglas, from Scotland, found his first specimen near the mouth of the Columbia river in 1825. Originally spelled *Douglass*, the name was Anglicized over time. This squirrel was almost known as the *Townsend squirrel*, after J.K. Townsend, who collected animals for John Bachman, John James Aububon's collaborator. But Bachman, who originally listed the squirrel with Townsend's name, accepted the other name in 1836 when he learned that Douglass's discovery had predated Townsends. In 1847, another early classification of this squirrel labelled it as *Sciurus californicus*, named after the location where one was spotted, and then renamed *Sciurus hudsonius* [sic] *californicus* because it was erroneously thought to be a subspecies of the red squirrel.

WESTERN GRAY SQUIRREL   *Sciurus griseus*
Griseus is the Latin word for gray, but is also a term sometimes used to describe a grizzled color in animal fur, characterized by mixed light and dark hair. The first published record of this squirrel was in 1818.

ABERT'S SQUIRREL   *Sciurus aberti*
The Abert's squirrel, also referred to as the tassel-eared squirrel, was named after Col. J.J. Abert, a naturalist and military officer who observed and recorded information about western wildlife in the early 1800s. The first published description of this squirrel was in 1852 by Dr. S.W.

Woodhouse, who encountered the animal while participating in the Sitgreaves exploration of the Colorado and Zuni Rivers. The *Kaibab squirrel*, a subspecies of the tassel-eared squirrel, is named after the geographic region it is associated with, the Kaibab plateau on the north rim of the Grand Canyon in Arizona.

FOX SQUIRREL   *Sciurus niger*

Niger is a Latin word meaning black or dark, one of the three color phases of the fox squirrel. Because the predominate color of its fur, at least in one of its color phases, was similar to the red fox, this squirrel was commonly called the fox squirrel. The first published record of this squirrel was in 1758 from an observation thought to have occurred in the southern part of South Carolina.

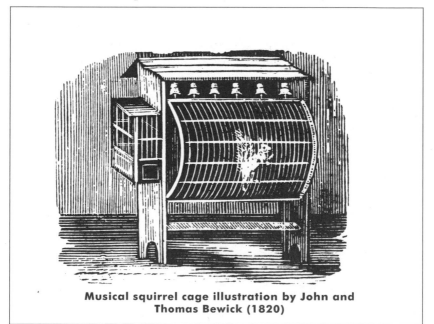

Musical squirrel cage illustration by John and Thomas Bewick (1820)

SQUIRREL SPECIES

Eastern gray squirrel   26

Western gray squirrel   30

Fox squirrel   34

Red squirrel   38

Douglas squirrel   42

Southern flying squirrel   46

Northern flying squirrel   50

Abert's squirrel   54

Arizona gray squirrel   58

COMPARING SQUIRREL SIZES

FOX SQUIRREL

ABERT'S SQUIRREL

GRAY SQUIRREL

RED SQUIRREL
DOUGLAS SQUIRREL

SOUTHERN FLYING
SQUIRREL

NORTHERN FLYING
SQUIRREL

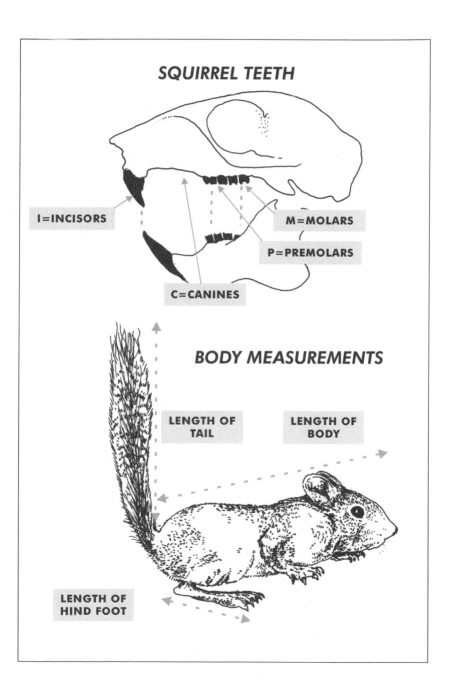

SQUIRREL TEETH

I=INCISORS

M=MOLARS

P=PREMOLARS

C=CANINES

BODY MEASUREMENTS

LENGTH OF TAIL

LENGTH OF BODY

LENGTH OF HIND FOOT

EASTERN GRAY SQUIRREL

Sciurus carolinensis

VITAL STATISTICS

OFFICIAL NAME	Eastern gray squirrel *Sciurus carolinensis*
COMMON NAMES	Carolina gray squirrel, black squirrel, migratory squirrel, cat squirrel, timber squirrel, silvertail
SUBSPECIES	Albino colonies in several states (Illinois, New Jersey, Ohio, S. Carolina). Subspecies include: *S.c. pennsylvanicus; S.c. hypophaeus; S.c. matecumbei; S.c. fuliginosus; S.c. extimus; S.c. carolinensis*
COMPARISON	Not as large as fox squirrel; fox squirrel has tail hairs with yellowish ends. Gray squirrel has white tips on tail guard hairs. Tail not as fluffy as fox squirrel. Ears larger and more pointed than fox squirrel.
DESCRIPTION	Mixed dark and light hairs in coat ("salt and pepper" pattern), colors from gray, tan or light brown to dark brown and black. Belly light, from white to gray. Tips of guard hairs in tail are white. White patches may be present behind ears in northern range. Individual squirrels may be all black, all gray, or all white. Bodies larger and heavier to the north. Molting occurs twice a year, in Spring and Fall.

BODY LENGTH	16 7/8-21″ 385-530 mm	**TAIL LENGTH**	8 1/4-10″ 150-250 mm
WEIGHT	12-26 oz 338-750 gm	**HINDFOOT LENGTH**	2-3″ 53-76 mm
TEETH	22 teeth I 1/1, C 0/0, P 2/1, M 3/3		

HOME RANGE	Mississippi River basin east to coast; Gulf coast north to Canada; Westernmost range from North Dakota south to Texas. Introduced in California, Oregon, Washington, and Montana.
HABITAT	Hardwood forests. Mature forests with dense undergrowth are preferred. Adapted to a variety of wooded conditions, including parks and urban areas, especially around oak and hickory trees.
FOOD	Acorns, nuts, seeds, buds, berries, inner bark, fungi, insects, animal bones and antlers. Carrion, birds' eggs, and nestling birds may be eaten, but less frequently than by red squirrels. Food is stored by scatter hoarding. Most food is carried away from gathering sites to be eaten or buried.
BREEDING	Two mating seasons per year with 2 litters common. Gestation period: 44-46 days. Birth: spring and late summer. Average litter size: 3. Young weigh 0.5-0.6 oz (14-18 gm). Weaning: 8-9 weeks. Sexually mature: 10-11 months.
NESTS	Nests in tree cavities or leaf nests high in trees. Generally prefers tree cavities in natural habitats. Nests large, leafy constructions spherical in shape. Summer nesting platforms smaller, flattened.
VOCAL CALL	Raspy "CRRK CRRK CRRK" or "QUACK QUACK QUACK" similar to a duck.
HABITS	Individual squirrels may move in fall months. Mass movements may occur sporadically, usually in fall months. Primary complaints: destruction of garden plants, trees; physical damage to buildings and wiring from gnawing; consumption of bird feed.
PREDATORS	Raptors, foxes, raccoons, bobcats, tree-climbing snakes.

RANGE FOR EASTERN GRAY SQUIRREL

The eastern gray squirrel has expanded well beyond its natural range because of human interaction. Established colonies of these common tree squirrels are now found in many cities in western and Pacific coast states. Gray squirrels have also been imported into Great Britain where they have taken over much of the traditional range of the European red squirrel.

WESTERN GRAY SQUIRREL

Sciurus griseus

VITAL STATISTICS

OFFICIAL NAME	Western gray squirrel *Sciurus griseus*
COMMON NAMES	California gray squirrel
SUBSPECIES	*S.g. anthonyi, S.g. griseus, S.g. nigripes.*
COMPARISON	Douglas squirrel is smaller with yellow or reddish belly. Fox squirrel is larger with yellowish or rusty coloring and smaller ears.
DESCRIPTION	Gray with white hairs. Belly lighter, white to light gray. Some red, yellow, or brown coloration common in upper body or backs of ears. Tail frequently banded with gray, white, and black. Body has distinct separation between coloring on back and on belly. Tail is large and bushy, broader than eastern gray squirrel. Feet may be dark colored. White circle around eyes. Bottoms of feet are gray. *Nigripes* subspecies has distinctive black hind paws.

BODY LENGTH	171/2-23 1/4" 510-579 mm	**TAIL LENGTH**	9 3/8-12 1/4" 265-290 mm
WEIGHT	12-34 oz 340-964 gm	**HINDFOOT LENGTH**	3-4" 74-80 mm

TEETH	22 teeth I 1/1, C 0/0, P 2/1, M 3/3
HOME RANGE	Pacific Coast states, Baja California in Mexico north to Canada through California, Oregon, and Washington.
HABITAT	Forested areas of redwoods and other conifers, or mixed hardwoods and conifers. Usually prefers elevations between 3,000-8,000 feet.

FOOD	Acorns, pine cones, nuts, bark, fruit, berries, fungi, insects. Food storage by scatter hoarding but less hoarding in general than eastern gray squirrel.
BREEDING	Breeding season: January-May. One litter per year; 2 litters possible. 2-5 young per litter. Gestation period: 44-46 days.
NESTS	Tree cavities or nests of leaves, bark, small branches, moss, and lichen. Placement high in trees. Usually builds large, bulky nests. May use nests of birds, especially crows or eagles.
VOCAL CALL	Raspy "CRRK CRRK CRRK" or "QUACK QUACK QUACK" similar to a duck.
HABITS	Spends more time foraging on the ground than the eastern gray squirrel. Group migrations may occur. Primary complaints: destruction of orchard crops (almonds, filberts, walnuts) and damage to young redwoods by bark stripping.
PREDATORS	Raptors, bobcats, foxes, coyotes, martens, house cats.

RANGE OF THE WESTERN GRAY SQUIRREL

FOX SQUIRREL

Sciurus niger

COLOR PHASE VARIATION

VITAL STATISTICS

OFFICIAL NAME	Fox squirrel *Sciurus niger*
COMMON NAMES	Sherman's fox squirrel, mangrove fox squirrel, cat squirrel, stump-eared squirrel
SUBSPECIES	*S.n. avicennia, S.n. bachmani, S.n. cinereus, S.n. limitis, S.n. ludovicianus, S.n. niger, S.n. rufiventer, S.n. shermania, S.n. subauratus, S.n. vulpinus*
COMPARISON	Larger than other tree squirrels. Black color phase differentiated from Abert's squirrel by distinctive ear tufts on Abert's. The Nayarit squirrel is a related species, but is found only in southeastern Arizona in the Chiricahua Mountains. Ears are shorter and more rounded than gray squirrel. Tail is larger and fluffier in gray.
DESCRIPTION	Largest tree squirrel. Coat is typically reddish brown with a lighter belly. 3 color phases: gray over yellow; reddish brown; black. Color variations may include white markings with white on face and white tip of tail, white ears, white nose, and black head. White or light-colored individuals common. Tail is typically mixed colors except in black color phase. Bottoms of feet are black. Tail bushy and often with yellow tips on tail hairs. Two molts annually, Spring and Fall. Bones distinctively pink.

BODY LENGTH	17 7/8-27 1/2" 454-698 mm	**TAIL LENGTH**	7 7/8-13" 200-330 mm
WEIGHT	17 5/8-37 1/8 oz 504-1062 gm	**HINDFOOT LENGTH**	2-3 1/4" 51-82 mm
TEETH	20 teeth I 1/1, C 0/0, P 1/1, M 3/3		

HOME RANGE	Eastern Rocky Mountains east to East Coast, Gulf Coast north to Canada; not present in New England; rare in New Jersey, parts of New York, Pennsylvania. Introduced in western states, including California, Montana, Oregon, and Washington.
HABITAT	Hardwood forests, sometimes found in conifers. In south, prefers conifers, especially longleaf pine and slash pine. Generally prefers less dense areas featuring open spaces, light undergrowth, and transitions between pastures or cropland and woods. Also present in mangrove and cypress swamps in the south.
FOOD	Acorns, pine cones, nuts, seeds, berries, fruit, buds, inner bark, wild gourds, bulbs, fungi, insects, bird eggs. Food storage by scatter hoarding. Carries food to eating perches; ground litter distinctive.
BREEDING	Mating period usually begins in late December. Birth: February-March, June-August. 2 litters per year; 2-4 young per litter. Average litter size: 3. Gestation period: 44-46 days. Young weigh 0.5-0.6 oz (14-18 gm). Sexually mature: 10-11 months.
NESTS	Typically uses nests in summer and tree cavities in winter. Known to share nests in winter.
VOCAL CALL	"CHUCK CHUCK CHUCK," deeper and slower than gray squirrel.
HABITS	Moves faster and with greater agility on the ground than gray. Individuals may change locations in fall. Primary complaints: destruction of garden and field crops, especially corn, tomatoes, strawberries, soybeans and orchard crops (pecans, English walnuts, avocados, oranges).
PREDATORS	Raptors, bobcats, weasels, snakes.

RANGE FOR FOX SQUIRREL

Fox squirrels have been introduced outside their natural range, especially in cities and parks in California, Montana, Oregon, and Washington.

RED SQUIRREL
Tamiasciurus hudsonicus

VITAL STATISTICS

OFFICIAL NAME	Red squirrel *Tamiasciurus hudsonicus*
COMMON NAMES	Chickaree, pine squirrel, spruce squirrel, barking squirrel, boomer, chatterbox, fairydiddle, rusty squirrel, rod robber, egg-eater
SUBSPECIES	*T.h. abieticola, T.h. baileyi, T.h. columbiensis, T.h. dakotensis, T.h. dixiensis, T.h. fremonti, T.h. grahamensis, T.h. gymnicus, T.h. hudsonicus, T.h. kenaiensis, T.h. lanuginosus, T.h. laurentianus, T.h. loquax, T.h. lychnuchus, T.h. minnesota, T.h. mogollonensis, T.h. pallescens, T.h. petulans, T.h. picatus, T.h. preblei, T.h. regalis, T.h. richardsoni, T.h. streatori, T.h. ungavensis, T.h. ventorum*
COMPARISON	About half the size of gray squirrel. Douglas squirrels have darker bellies. Hair tufts on ears much smaller than in tassel-eared squirrels but more pronounced than in gray and fox squirrels. Tail smaller and flatter than gray and fox squirrels.
DESCRIPTION	Body reddish brown or rust, tan, gray, yellowish, or reddish with pale to white belly. Darker band laterally on sides between back and belly. White ring around eye. Tail hairs feature darker stripe on outside edges with line of white. Small hair tufts on ears. Tail hairs have yellowish tips; tail has dark border. Seasonal variations: paler color on back in Winter; dark line along sides between back and belly in Summer. Two molts annually, Spring and Fall.

BODY LENGTH	10 5/8-151/4″ 270-385 mm	**TAIL LENGTH**	3 5/8-6 1/4″ 92-158 mm

WEIGHT	5-11 oz 145-260 gm	HINDFOOT LENGTH	1 3/8-2 1/4" 35-57 mm
TEETH	22 teeth I 1/1, C 0/0, P 2/1, M 3/3		
HOME RANGE	Canada and northern U.S., Rocky Mountain states south through Arizona and New Mexico. Common in New England and midwest from eastern North Dakota through the Atlantic coast, south through the Appalachians.		
HABITAT	Deciduous and conifer forests, prefers conifers.		
FOOD	Pine cones, acorns, nuts, buds, fruit, seeds, sap, berries, fungi, bark, birds' eggs, nestlings, small mammals (including young rabbits, gray squirrels), carrion, bones and antlers. Corn is also a regular part of the diet. Food storage by larder hoarding.		
BREEDING	Mating: late winter. Birth: March-April, August-September. One litter annually: 3-7 young per litter. Two litters possible. Gestation period: 35 days. Young average weight: 0.3 oz (7.5 gm). Eyes open 27-35 days. Sexually mature: 10-12 months.		
NESTS	Nests in tree cavities, leaf nests, abandoned birds' nests, or underground cavities. Prefers leaf nests, built of shredded bark, grass, and leaves. Often nest in conifers.		
VOCAL CALL	High-pitched "TCHK TCHK TCHK" or chatter.		
HABITS	Very active, more aggressive than other tree squirrels. Territory is maintained by aggressive displays. Negative factors: bark stripping and eating of buds is commercially damaging to some timber trees, including birch, Norway spruce, white spruce, and white pine.		
PREDATORS	Raptors, foxes, martens, lynx.		

RANGE FOR RED SQUIRREL

DOUGLAS SQUIRREL
Tamiasciurus douglasii

VITAL STATISTICS

OFFICIAL NAME	Douglas squirrel *Tamiasciurus douglasii*
COMMON NAMES	Chickaree, pine squirrel, Douglas chickaree, yellow-breasted pine squirrel, yellow-belly, piney sprite, yellow piney
SUBSPECIES	*T.d. albolimbatus, T.d. doyuglasii, T.d. mollipilosus, T.d. mearnsi*
COMPARISON	More gray and brown color on back than red squirrel. Belly not as white as red squirrel and with yellow tint. Smaller than gray and fox squirrels. Hair tufts not as long as tassel-eared squirrel, but more pronounced than gray and fox squirrels.
DESCRIPTION	Body rust, olive brown, or reddish brown to gray; belly yellow to orange. Darker stripe laterally on sides between back and belly. Tail features dark to black end with underside rust or reddish brown and dark band on edges with some white hairs. Small ear tufts, dark colored. White ring around eye. Seasonal variations: dark band along sides in Summer; ears have longer tufts in Winter. Two molts annually, Spring and Fall.

BODY LENGTH	10 5/8-14" 270-345 mm	**TAIL LENGTH**	3 7/8-6 1/8" 102-156 mm
WEIGHT	51/4-10 1/2 oz 150-300 gm	**HINDFOOT LENGTH**	1 3/4-2 1/4" 44-55 mm

TEETH	22 teeth I 1/1, C 0/0, P 2/1, M 3/3
HOME RANGE	Pacific coast from British Columbia (west of the Coast Range) south through northern California; also south through the Sierra Mountains to northern part of Baja California in Mexico. Docs not share territory with the red squirrel.

HABITAT	Coniferous forests preferred but may occur in deciduous forests. Found from sea level to about 6,000 feet. Prefers dense conifer coverage, but may move into secondary growth areas. Also known to nest and forage in rocky terrain where trees are scarce.
FOOD	Pine cones, acorns, nuts, fungi, buds, fruits, berries, birds' eggs, nestling birds, carrion, bone and antlers. Food storage by larder hoarding. Uses caches for cones, nuts, and fungi. Feeds in selected spots, forming piles of discarded material (middens).
BREEDING	Mating period: early spring. One litter per year; may have second litter. Birth: May-June. Litter size: 4-6. Gestation period: 33 days.
NESTS	Prefers leaf nests but may use tree cavities or hollow trees. Nests built from leaves, bark, small branches, moss, lichen.
VOCAL CALL	High-pitched "TCHK TCHK" similar to red squirrel, but often in two-note, two-tone pairs.
HABITS	Noisy, active, similar to red squirrel. Aggressive and defends territory. Negative factors: can cause damage to seedlings and restricts reseeding cycles.
PREDATORS	Raptors, martens, bobcats, fishers, lynx, weasel, mink.

RANGE FOR DOUGLAS SQUIRREL

SOUTHERN FLYING SQUIRREL

Glaucomys volans

VITAL STATISTICS

OFFICIAL NAME	Southern flying squirrel *Glaucomys volans*
COMMON NAMES	Eastern flying squirrel, white-furred flying squirrel, little flying squirrel, glider, fairydiddle
SUBSPECIES	*G.v. saturatu, G.v. texensis, G.v. underwoodi, G.v. volans*
COMPARISON	Smaller than the northern flying squirrel. Distinct from other tree squirrels because of the flap of skin used to glide. Also, the flying squirrel's whiskers are more prominent, and the ears are larger in proportion to the head than the other squirrels.
DESCRIPTION	Smallest tree squirrel. Gray, olive, light brown, or brown with a white to cream-colored belly. Black ring around the eye. Presence of the patagium, a flap of skin used to glide. The patagium connects the front leg to the back leg from the wrist to the ankle. Gliding membrane has dark or black outside border. Very large eyes; ears large in proportion to head. Tail flattened. In southern range, color is darker. Seasonal variation: toes white in Winter. One molt per year, in Fall.

BODY LENGTH	5-6" 125-175 mm	**TAIL LENGTH**	3-5" 75-120 mm
WEIGHT	1.4-3.5 oz 40-98 gm	**HINDFOOT LENGTH**	3/4-1 1/3" 21-33 mm
TEETH	22 teeth I 1/1, C 0/0, P 2/1, M 3/3		

HOME RANGE	Eastern North America; Gulf Coast north to Ontario; East coast to midwest, west to northeast corner of Nebraska; Missouri River basin. Range overlaps that of the northern flying squirrel in some areas. Missing in New England.
HABITAT	Deciduous forests, mostly oak, hickory, beech, maple, and mixed deciduous-conifer. Prefers wooded areas with adequate number of dead trees for nesting.
FOOD	Acorns, nuts, berries, bark, fruit, buds, beetles, moths, other insects, birds' eggs, small vertebrates, carrion. Uses larder hoarding; may store food in nest.
BREEDING	Mating: early spring. Breeding periods: February-March, May-July. 2 litters per year. Litter size: 2-6. Gestation period: 40 days. Weaning: 6-8 weeks. Sexual maturity: 12 months.
NESTS	Nests in hollow cavities in trees. Prefers cavities 15-20 feet above ground. In summer may build nest of leaves, bark, and small branches. Congregates in groups for nesting during winter months (up to fifty have been found in one nest).
VOCAL CALL	High-pitched "CHWEEP CHWEEP CHWEEP." Whistle-like call similar to that of a bird.
HABITS	Nocturnal. Can glide up to 150 feet. More aggressive than the northern flying squirrel. Traditionally kept as pets in some areas. Does not hibernate but may remain inactive for days in the extreme cold.
PREDATORS	Raptors, martens, mink, weasels, raccoons, snakes, house cats.

RANGE FOR SOUTHERN FLYING SQUIRREL

NORTHERN FLYING SQUIRREL

Glaucomys sabrinus

VITAL STATISTICS

OFFICIAL NAME	Northern flying squirrel *Glaucomys sabrinus*
COMMON NAMES	Mearn's flying squirrel, big flying squirrel, Canadian flying squirrel
SUBSPECIES	*G.s. alpinus, G.s. bangsi, G.s. californicus, G.s. canescens, G.s. coloratus, G.s. columbiensis, G.s. flaviventris, G.s. fuliginosus, G.s. fuscus, G.s. goodwini, G.s. gouldi, G.s. griseifrons, G.s. klamathensis, G.s. lascivus, G.s. latipes, G.s. lucifugus, G.s. macrotis, G.s. makkovikensis, G.s. oregonensis, G.s. reductus, G.s. sabrinus, G.s. stephensi, G.s. yukonensis, G.s. zaphaeus*
COMPARISON	Larger than southern flying squirrel. Hair on belly is white only on tips. Color is generally brighter.
DESCRIPTION	Brown with lighter to white belly. Presence of patagium, a flap of skin used for gliding. The patagium connects the front leg to the back leg from the wrist to the ankle. Gliding membrane has dark or black outside border. In southern range, coloration is darker. Tail is flattened. Feet light colored underneath. Seasonal variation: lighter color and small ear tufts, soles of feet furred in winter. One molt per year, in Fall.

BODY LENGTH	10 3/8-14 1/2" 263-368 mm	**TAIL LENGTH**	4 1/2-7 1/8" 115-180 mm
WEIGHT	1 5/8-5 oz 45-140 gm	**HINDFOOT LENGTH**	1 1/3-1 3/4" 34-45 mm
TEETH	22 teeth　I 1/1, C 0/0, P 2/1, M 3/3		

HOME RANGE	Alaska east throughout Canada, northwest territories south through northern U.S. Rocky Mountains; upper Great Lakes from Minnesota east to New York; New England; Appalachian range.
HABITAT	Deciduous and conifer forests, also in mixed deciduous-conifer woods. Found from sea level to about 6,000 feet. Generally prefers conifers.
FOOD	Acorns, nuts, seeds, berries, lichens, fungi, buds, fruit, insects, birds' eggs, nestlings, small birds, small mammals, carrion. Larder hoarding; may cache food in piles near bases of trees. Attracted to sweet tree sap, especially maple.
BREEDING	Mating: late winter. Birth: spring. Litter size: 2-5. May have second litter in late summer. Gestation period: 37-42 days. Young weigh 6 gm. Weaning: 45-65 days. First gliding: 3 months.
NESTS	Nests in tree cavities. In summer may make nests from twigs and strips of bark or use abandoned bird nests or nests of other tree squirrels.
VOCAL CALL	High-pitched "CHWEEP CHWEEP CHWEEP." Whistle-like call similar to that of a bird. Calls lower pitched than southern flying squirrel.
HABITS	Nocturnal. Uses skin flaps to glide up to 150 feet. Not as aggressive as southern flying squirrel. May be threatened or endangered in southern range as a result of competition from southern flying squirrel, logging, and urbanization of prime habitat.
PREDATORS	Raptors, bobcats, lynx, martens, fishers, weasels, tree-climbing snakes, house cats.

RANGE OF NORTHERN FLYING SQUIRREL

ABERT'S SQUIRREL

Sciurus aberti

ALTERNATE COLOR PHASE

VITAL STATISTICS

OFFICIAL NAME	Abert's squirrel *Sciurus aberti*
COMMON NAMES	Tassel-eared squirrel
SUBSPECIES	Kaibab squirrel (*S.c. aberti kaibabensis*), subspecies living only in the vicinty of the south rim of the Grand Canyon in Arizona. Other subspecies: *S.a. aberti, S.a. barberi, S.a. chuscensis, S.a. durangi, S.a. ferreus, S.a. mimus, S.a. navajo, S.a. phaeurus*
COMPARISON	About the size of the gray squirrel but ear tufts are unique, extending up to 1".
DESCRIPTION	Large size. Ears most distinctive characteristic: large with vertical tufts of hair. Ears up to 1 3/4" (44 mm) with tufts up to 1" (25 mm). Tufts grow longer with age. Dark brown or black, sides darker, grizzled coloring common. 3 color phases: dark gray body with black lateral line and white belly, gray tail fringed with white; all black including tail; brown including tail. Kaibab squirrel distinguished by dark coloring with a white tail. Seasonal variation: darker band laterally between back and belly and longer ear tufts.

BODY LENGTH	18 1/4-23" 463-584 mm	**TAIL LENGTH**	7 1/4-10" 195-255 mm
WEIGHT	1 1/2-2 lb 681-908 gm	**HINDFOOT LENGTH**	2 1/2-3 1/8" 65-80 mm
TEETH	22 teeth I 1/1, C 0/0, P 2/1, M 3/3		

HOME RANGE	Arizona, Colorado, New Mexico, Utah, Wyoming (also in Chihuahua and Durango, Mexico). Kaibab squirrel limited to north rim of the Grand Canyon in Arizona.
HABITAT	Higher elevations above 6,000 feet in mountainous areas. Yellow pine and ponderosa pine woods, up to about 8,500 feet in elevation. Prefers ponderosa pine, may also live in juniper and pinyon habitats.
FOOD	Pine cones (primarily ponderosa pine, pinyon pine, spruce), berries, inner bark, buds, pine flowers, mistletoe, fruit, fungi, carrion, acorns. Food cached by scatter hoarding.
BREEDING	Mating: February-March. Males compete for females with a mating bout and chase. One litter per year; two litters possible. Litter size: 3-4. Gestation period: 38-46 days. Birth weight: 12 gm. Weaning: 10 weeks. Sexual maturity: 10-11 months.
NESTS	Nests made of branches, twigs, and leaves. Nests built 15-90 feet above ground next to trunk, up to 3 feet in diameter. May use dwarf mistletoe (witches broom) growths as nesting sites.
VOCAL CALL	Low clucks and barks, "CHUCK CHUCK CHUCK," similar to fox squirrel.
HABITS	Generally nonaggressive.
PREDATORS	Raptors, coyotes.

RANGE FOR ABERT'S SQUIRREL

VITAL STATISTICS	
OFFICIAL NAME	Arizona gray squirrel *Sciurus arizonensis*
COMMON NAME	Arizona gray squirrel
SUBSPECIES	*S.a. arizonensis, S.a. catalinac, S.a. huachuca*
DESCRIPTION	Uniform gray with lighter belly. Tail has fringe of white. Tops of feet gray. Seasonal variation: darker band laterally between back and belly in winter, body grayer in winter. Summer coat may be stained darker brown from walnut juice, a distinctive temporary marking. Although considered a separate species of gray squirrel, may be more closely related to the fox squirrel.
HOME RANGE	Limited regions of southwestern Arizona and western New Mexico.
HABITAT	Lowlands, valleys, and canyons. Deciduous forests (walnut, sycamore, cottonwood) or mixed diciduous-conifer forests. Generally prefers elevations from 4,000-8,000 feet.

TAXONOMY

"In their quick graceful motions from branch to branch, they almost remind one of a bird, and they are always neat and cleanly in their coats, industrious, and well provided for the cold of winter." — John James Audubun

In the science of classification, taxonomists work to understand the relationship among plants and animals by defining their differences. In this scheme, squirrels are classified as members of the rodent order, one of fourteen orders of mammals and the largest group among all mammals. The squirrel family is one of 31 families of rodents and consists of about 250 different species, including chipmunks and marmots. Squirrels are classified by their scientific name: *sciuridae*, a Latin designation originally taken from the Greek words meaning "shadow tail."

The characteristics of rodents include a pair of long teeth at the front of both the upper and lower jaws. These incisors are chisel-shaped and form a shallow curve. All rodents experience continual growth of these teeth throughout their lives, necessitating constant gnawing on hard objects in order to keep them from growing too long for easy use. Gnawing wears away these incisors in a chisel-like fashion because only the front surface has a hard enamel coat. Behind the enamel is a softer dentine material which is worn away through use. In fact, the name rodent is derived from the Latin word rodere, meaning "to gnaw." Rodents are the ultimate "gnawing animal." Squirrel incisors grow about six inches a year.

There is also a distinctive gap between the incisors of rodents and their set of grinding teeth. As members of the rodent order, squirrels share this incisor characteristic. Other distinctive features are listed on page 63.

WORLD MAMMALS

ORDER	DESCRIPTION	No. OF SPECIES	No. OF FAMILIES
MONOTREMES	platypus and spiny anteater	3	2
MARSUPIALIA	opossums, bandicoots, kangaroos, wombats, and other marsupials	265	15
INSECTIVORA	hedgehogs, moles, shrews	406	9
CHIROPTERA	bats	879	18
RODENTIA	rodents	1625	31
EDENTATA	anteaters, tree sloths, armadillos	28	3
LAGOMORPHA	rabbits, hares, pikas	60	2
CARNIVORA	dogs, foxes, wolves, seals, weasels, cats, and other carnivores	266	9
CETACEA	whales, dolphins, porpoises	76	10
PROBOSCIDEA	elephants	2	1
SIRENIA	dugongs, manatees	4	2
PERISSODACTYLA	horses, zebras, tapirs, rhinoceroses	16	3
ARTOPDACTYLA	antelope, deer, gazelles, giraffe, pigs, hippos, and other ruminants	185	9
PRIMATES	lemurs, monkeys, apes, humans	199	15

THE SQUIRREL
SUBORDER OF RODENTS

**SCALY-TAILED
SQUIRRELS**

**TREE
SQUIRRELS**

BEAVERS

SPRINGHARES

**POCKET
GOPHERS**

**MOUNTAIN
BEAVERS**

**KANGAROO
RATS**

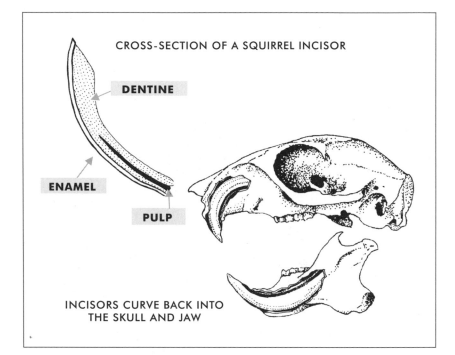

CROSS-SECTION OF A SQUIRREL INCISOR

DENTINE

ENAMEL

PULP

INCISORS CURVE BACK INTO
THE SKULL AND JAW

DEFINITIONS

MAMMALS   *Animals with spinal columns (vertebrates) that have hair and the females have mammary glands that produce milk.*

RODENTS   *Mammals that have unique incisors that are used for gnawing.*

— four toes on front feet; five toes on back feet
— masseter muscle, the main muscle used to work the jaw, extends forward along the side of the snout and compresses the infraorbital foramen. Postorbital process of frontal separates the eye from the temporal muscle. "Incisor enamel uniserial."
— tail always covered with hair
— Dental formula: Incisors: upper 1-1; lower 1-1
           Canines: upper 0-0; lower 0-0
           Premolars: upper 1-1; lower 1-1 (exception: upper is 2-2 for *Marmota, Sciurus aberti, S. carolinensis, S. griseus, Tamiasciurus*)
           Molars: upper 3-3; lower 3-3
— total teeth: 20 (exception: 22 for *Marmota, S. aberti, S. carolinensis, S. griseus, Tamiasciurus*)

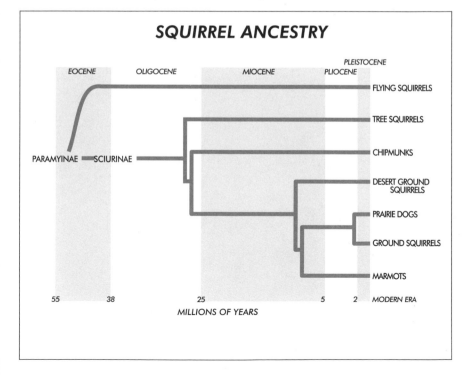

SQUIRREL ANCESTRY

Squirrels are found throughout the world with a few exceptions. No squirrels are native to Australia, Madagascar, and Antarctica. From continent to continent, squirrels look more or less like what is seen on the American continent, but size, color, and a few unique characteristics make some foreign squirrels stand apart.

WORLD SQUIRRELS

AFRICAN BUSH SQUIRREL

WEST AFRICAN SUN SQUIRREL

EUROPEAN RED SQUIRREL

GIANT FLYING SQUIRREL

In England and Europe, the red squirrel is the only tree squirrel native to that continent. Gray squirrels from North America were transplanted in England beginning in the late 1800s and have established a dominance over the native red squirrels, eliminating them from much of their original range and creating problems for some trees through bark stripping. In recent years, flying squirrels are also arriving in Great Britain, imported as pets to a country with none of its own. The European red squirrel (*Sciurus vulgaris*) is larger than the American red squirrel and has large ear tufts, similar to the North American Abert's squirrel. In recent years, flying squirrels from North America have also been imported into England as pets.

In Pakistan, the Woolly flying squirrel is the largest living member of the squirrel family. Once thought to be extinct, recent sightings are helping to provide a better understanding of this animal. Up to two feet long with a tail that is another two feet, the Woolly flying squirrel (*Eupetaurus cinereus*) lives high in the mountains. This squirrel has a legendary status: its crystallized urine is sought after as an aphrodisiac.

In Africa, native squirrels include the pygmy squirrel (*Myosciurus pumilio*), only about 5 inches in length; the African giant squirrel (*Protoxerus stangeri*); a dozen varieties of African bush squirrels (Paroxerus); and the sun squirrel (*Heliosciurus*). Asian squirrels include the palm squirrels (*Funambulus*), and many species of Oriental tree squirrels (*Callosciurus*). One of the largest tree squirrels in the world, the Indian giant squirrel (*Ratufa indica*), up to 3 feet in length, is native to India, Borneo, Java, and Sumatra. Species of flying squirrels are found in Europe (the Polatouche, or European flying squirrel) and Asia (the red and white flying squirrel).

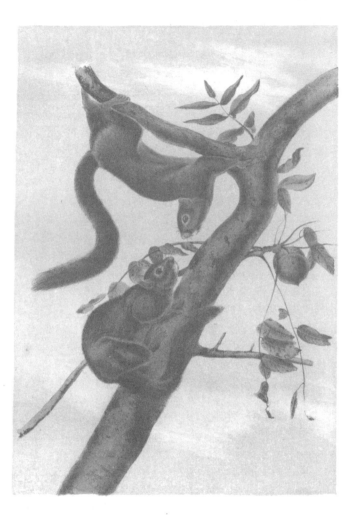

John Audubon and his collaborator, John Bachman, originally described several native squirrels as new species, including this one, which they called the "Orange-bellied Squirrel." Illustration by J. J. Audubon (*The Vivaporous Quadrapeds of North America*, 1851. Plate LVIII).

The ancestors of the modern squirrel have been traced back as far as the Miocene era, about 50 million years ago. Fossilized predecessors of squirrels are classified as the *paramyids*, the earliest known form of rodents. Paramyids varied in size from a few inches, the size of mice, to beaver-sized creatures. The beavers currently alive in the world are thought to be the nearest living relatives of those primitive mammals.

During the early periods of the Eocene, Paramys species began to feature incisors with the now-characteristic triangular shape and an enamel layer on the front.

"This appears to be the most active and sprightly species of Squirrel existing in our Atlantic States. It sallies forth with the sun, and is industriously engaged in search of food for four or five hours in the morning, scratching among leaves, running over fallen logs, ascending trees, or playfully skipping from bough to bough, often making almost incredible leaps from the higher branches of one tree to another. In the middle of the day it retires for a few hours to its nest, resuming its active labours and amusements in the afternoon, and continuing them without intermission till long after the setting of the sun."

— John James Audubon, John Bachman
The Vivaporous Quadrapeds of North America, 1851

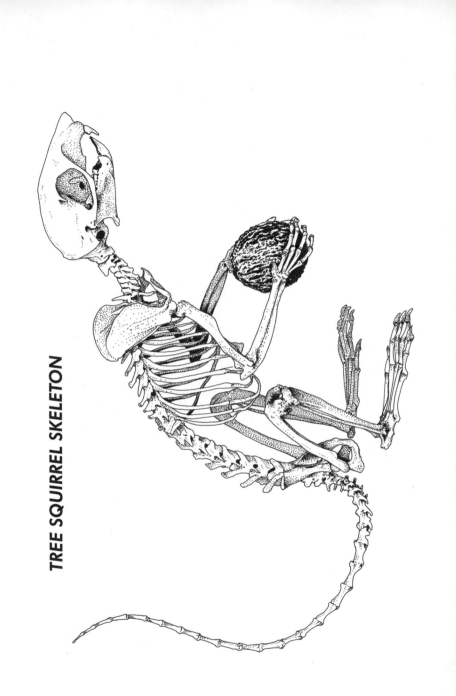

TREE SQUIRREL SKELETON

TREE SQUIRREL SKULL
(Sciurus carolinensis)

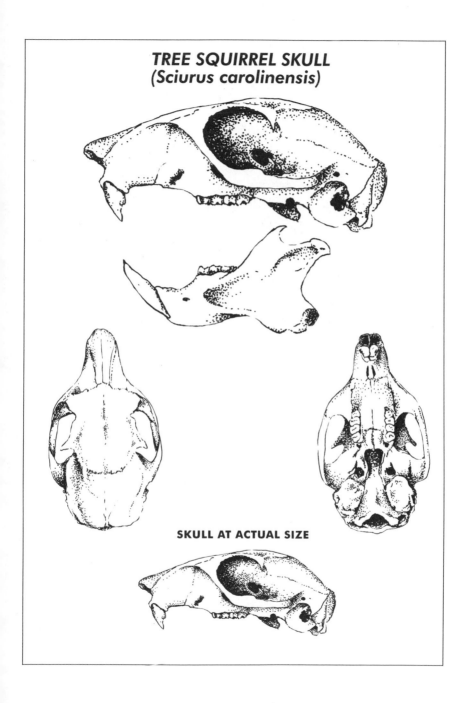

SKULL AT ACTUAL SIZE

Some Paramys species during the Eocene were physically similar to the squirrels of the present era except for size — the earlier versions were up to 24 inches (60 cm) in length — and some characteristics of the shape of the skull.

The family sciuridae includes about 250 species of squirrels. Because a single species of squirrel can have many different variations in coloring, it is often a challenge to the casual observer to determine what kind of creature they are watching. This problem can vex even experienced naturalists. When John James Audubon was illustrating the book, *The Vivaparous Quadruped of North America*, his collaborator, the Reverend John Bachman, wrote to him in 1839 to warn him of the difficulties.

"The animals have never been carefully described, and you will find difficulties at every step ... and the ever varying Squirrels seem sent by Satan himself, to puzzle the Naturalists."

Subsequently, although their work became the standard reference for many decades, several types of squirrels were indeed misnamed, with both Audubon and Bachman listing some regional variations of the fox and gray squirrels as separate species.

SQUIRREL ANATOMY

"Forth he comes in that bright hot spell; and, for four or five hours, prowls and plays the life game with the fullest measure of his gifts." — *Ernest Thompson Seton*

Tree squirrels are ideally adapted for life above the ground. Their bodies are light and flexible and their limbs and tails are efficient tools for clinging to vertical surfaces and maintaining balance.

TEETH

The primary characteristic of rodents, teeth are uniquely developed in each species for certain kinds of eating activity. With tree squirrels, gnawing hard substances such as nut shells is efficiently accomplished because of the chisel-shaped incisors in the upper and lower jaws. A hard coating of enamel on the front side only keeps them sharp as they are used because the softer material behind the enamel wears away faster.

After food is bitten off or shredded with the incisors, the squirrel's molars take over to grind it into a more digestible form. The gnawing action of the incisors is performed with an up-and-down motion while the lower jaw is pulled slightly forward to allow the front teeth to work together. The grinding of the molars is accomplished with a circular, side-to-side action as the lower jaw is pulled back slightly. Squirrels use their tongues to move food to the right place in their mouths and are very efficient at ejecting bits of undesirable elements such as shells.

EYES

Squirrels have a wide range of vision, useful in spotting predators. Their eyes are placed to allow clear visibility to the front and can also gather visual information from the sides and above without moving the eyes or head. Because the optic nerve enters the back of the eye, however, squirrels have a blind spot in their vision, a small horizontal area in the rear upper third of their vision.

Similar to the visual system of humans, squirrels can judge distances through parallax, the slight difference in focus allowed by the separation of the two eyes. Judging distance is critical because it allows them to locate appropriate landing spots when they jump from perch to perch above the ground. Squirrels often shift their head from side to side or up and down just before jumping, gathering additional visual information about the distance involved.

Squirrels also have the ability to focus clearly on distant objects. They may have vision as sharp as humans, in fact. In one study, squirrels were able to recognize other squirrels known to them from a distance of fifty feet.

Can squirrels detect color? Although the physiology of their eyes indicates it is possible, studies have shown that squirrels probably do not identify or react to differences in color, being able at most to distinguish only one or two. Instead, their vision uses variations in brightness to separate objects and pick up details. Flying squirrels have eyes adapted for maximum vision in the dark, although they are unable to see in complete darkness.

EARS

Although not dependent on their ears as the main source of information, squirrels do have an acute sense of hearing.

Sounds of predators and rival squirrels are important for their survival. Squirrels can move their ears to some extent, helping to focus on distant noises. A covering of fur protects them from the effects of cold temperatures; red squirrels, Abert's squirrels, and Douglas squirrels exhibit ear tufts that are usually longer in the winter.

SENSE OF SMELL

Squirrels have a highly-developed sense of smell which is an important tool in their quest for food. Buried caches, for instance, are located mostly by scent. Even under a layer of snow, squirrels are able to locate their stashes, although the process may be imperfect, leaving some nuts undetected.

Scents also allows squirrels to make important decisions about which nuts they select to harvest, cache, and eat. Many nuts are infested with natural pests — insects that have bored into the nutritious center. Squirrels detect the presence of

Scent marking is used on branches, tree trunks, stumps, and rocks or other objects on the ground.

WHITE SQUIRREL CENTRAL

Olney, Illinois, is one of the sites where a large colony of light-colored (albino) gray squirrels is found. According to local history, in 1902 a shopkeeper acquired a male and a female gray squirrel with the distinctive light coloring. On display in his shop window, they attracted attention and complaints from other store owners. After an ordinance was passed banning the display of live animals in store windows, the pair was released and has passed on their characteristics to succeeding generations of squirrels in the area. Currently there are several thousand of these white squirrels in the area and the town promotes them as a unique local symbol.

these pests through their sense of smell and either discard the infected nuts or eat them on the spot, adding the insect to the menu of the moment. Squirrels are so adept at selecting only healthy, unspoiled nuts that human nut collectors often seek out their hoards for raiding in order to improve the quality of their harvest.

Smell cues are also important in identifying and marking territory, both to protect it from rival squirrels and in the case of females, to attract mates at the appropriate time of year.

Urine is one fluid that squirrels can use to impart a scent message. There are also sweat and oil glands on the underside of their paws that can leave telltale odors. Squirrels can sometimes be seen "scooting" along branches, pulling themselves along with their forepaws, probably to leave a scent trail from their fur or oil glands. Female squirrels — and females of many other mammal species — have unique scent signals that are emitted when they are in estrus and ready to mate.

FUR

The specialized outer skin that has evolved on squirrels has an important role in their survival in a wide range of conditions. The fur keeps them warm and camouflaged.

Squirrels are born hairless. Their first coat of fur begins developing in only one or two weeks. For most adult tree squirrels, this coat is shed twice a year, in spring and fall molts. During a molt, successive parts of the body discard individual hairs, replacing them with a new generation. Typically, the spring molt starts at the head and progresses toward the rear; the fall molt starts at the rear and progresses toward the head. For most squirrels, slight seasonal variations in color and pattern are part of this molt. The molt takes place over a period of 4-6 weeks but is irregular in its timing with individual squirrels molting on different schedules. Hair on the tail and the ears may molt only once a year.

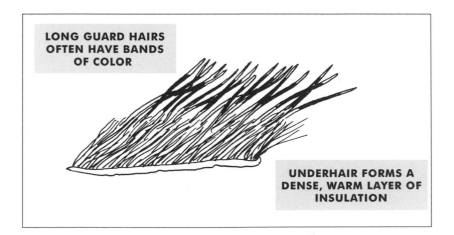

LONG GUARD HAIRS OFTEN HAVE BANDS OF COLOR

UNDERHAIR FORMS A DENSE, WARM LAYER OF INSULATION

Some squirrels also have fur on the bottom of their feet, although this may only grow during the winter months, protecting the feet against freezing surfaces.

Squirrel fur is multi-layered, similar to the fur of many mammals. Shorter inner hairs provide a thick, insulating mat that traps air and heat. The longer outer hairs — referred to as guard hairs — make up the visible coat. Individual guard hairs may be a single color or have different colors in bands on the shaft. Various patterns and tints provide effective camouflage. Red squirrels, for instance, are thought to have evolved their unique coloration because it closely resembles the pine tree litter on the floor of coniferous forests, the location where they do most of their foraging. The coats of gray squirrels more closely mimics the bark of hardwood trees.

All of the species of tree squirrels in North America have more than one coloring pattern. Variations exist from one extent of their range to another and migrations and mixed breeding provides a wide palette of possible combinations.

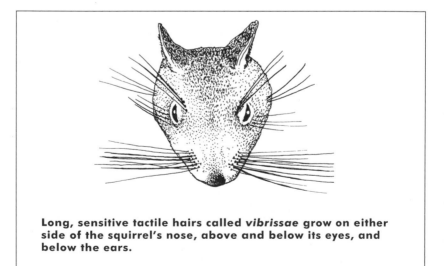

Long, sensitive tactile hairs called *vibrissae* grow on either side of the squirrel's nose, above and below its eyes, and below the ears.

This factor confused early naturalists (Audubon, for example, originally listed more than a dozen different specics for what is now recognized as one, the gray squirrel) and continues to befuddle many wildlife observers today. At its worst, in some regions the red squirrel may be gray or brown, and the gray squirrel red.

Distinctive groups of color variations are also part of the tree squirrels existence. Extremely dark groups of squirrels — referred to as melanistic forms — exist within the range of most tree squirrels and these often interbreed with "normally" colored members of their species, producing even wider variations in color.

True albino individuals also exist but are not as common as melanistic forms. Albino squirrels are characterized by a lack of pigment in their fur. In its extreme form, albino animals lack pigment even in their eyes, making them a distinctive pink color. Squirrels with albino characteristics may appear white or blond with normally colored eyes or have white patches on the bodies, limbs, or tails, a condition referred to as piebald (or skewbald) in some hoofed mammals. Several major colonies of light-colored gray squirrels have existed for decades in parts of their range.

A third kind of hair is also part of the fur. Specialized hairs on parts of the body do more than provide insulation. Extrasensitive hairs called *vibrissae* form whiskers that add additional sensory capabilities, of particular use to the squirrel in dark nests and tree cavities. Just as with other rodents, the whiskers, projecting several inches out from each side of their head, give them accurate feedback about the size of an opening they may wish to enter. Baby squirrels are born with these facial whiskers, a useful resource because they are also born blind and need help finding their mother's body in the nest. Squirrels have four sets altogether: one above the eyes, one below the eyes, one under the lower jaw, and the main set alongside the nose. Female squirrels also have a single tactile hair on each nipple (eight altogether).

Additional tactile hairs are located on the forepaws just above the wrists. These hairs provide a practical extension of the squirrels' versatile front paws while moving, flexing, and dexterously making selections of food.

FEET

Squirrels are characterized by the difference between their front and rear feet. The front feet have four digits; the rear feet have five digits. A vestigial "thumb" is present on the front paws. All these digits have permanent claws, one of the important features necessary to make the squirrel at home above the ground.

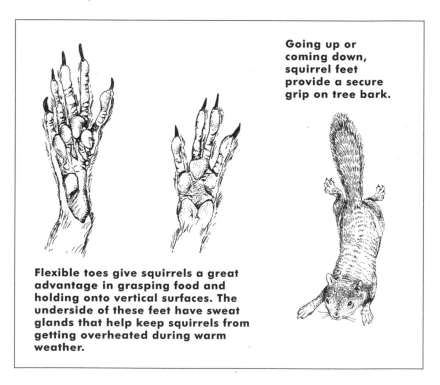

Going up or coming down, squirrel feet provide a secure grip on tree bark.

Flexible toes give squirrels a great advantage in grasping food and holding onto vertical surfaces. The underside of these feet have sweat glands that help keep squirrels from getting overheated during warm weather.

When descending a vertical surface, the squirrel can rotate its rear legs over a wide range. This allows the rear claws to effectively hook onto the surface, giving the squirrel a comfortable, stable position that allows rapid movement and the freedom to use its front paws in feeding even while inverted.

Although born hairless and blind, baby squirrels come into the world already equipped with their claws.

TAIL

The squirrel uses its tail for shade, protection from the elements, balance, warmth, and communications. The long, flexible appendage can also be used to control the body somewhat while jumping through the air. When jumping — or falling — to the ground from a height, squirrels may find their tails useful as partial parachutes, slowing their descent. Flying squirrels have flattened tails that are an important part of their gliding capability because the extra surface provides added braking and maneuverability in the air.

The underneath coloring and pattern of the tail can reveal information about the age of a squirrel. In gray squirrels, stripes mark juveniles; the stripes are not present in adults.

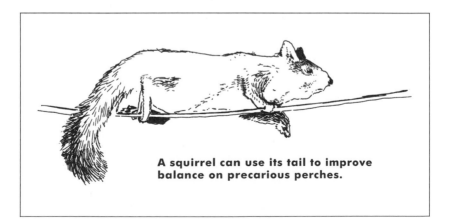

A squirrel can use its tail to improve balance on precarious perches.

Tails may also perform an odd protective function — distracting predators. Squirrels are frequently found with injured tails or with tails partially missing, the victim of missed attacks from the ground or the air. In one published record, a squirrel standing on the lip of a small pond was twitching its tail over the water, attracting the attentions of a fish in the pond. The fish attacked the tail as if it were a lure, stripping the fur from the flesh.

Under more typical circumstances, the squirrel's tail is an important tool in "body language." Depending on its position (curled over the body, straight up, or straight back) and action (motionless or flicking back and forth) the tail can signal fear, curiosity, friendly intentions, or anger.

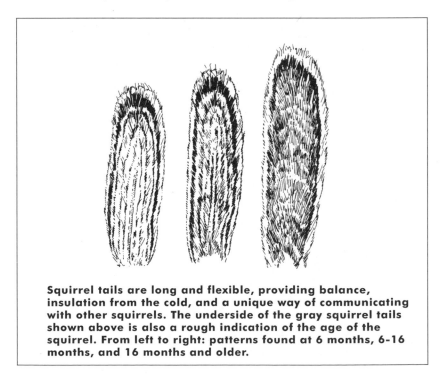

Squirrel tails are long and flexible, providing balance, insulation from the cold, and a unique way of communicating with other squirrels. The underside of the gray squirrel tails shown above is also a rough indication of the age of the squirrel. From left to right: patterns found at 6 months, 6-16 months, and 16 months and older.

DIET

"The squirrel on the shingly shagbark's bough
Now saws, now lists with downward eye and ear
Then drops his nut. " — James Russell Lowell

It is not by accident that squirrels are thought of as "nutty."
The relationship between squirrels and nuts is as critical as
that between beavers and aspen bark or timber wolves and
elk. Although these animals all have a varied diet, a strong
and continuous balance has evolved between each and its
favorite food. For tree squirrels in North America, a much
different lifestyle would have evolved without the presence
of a widespread natural supermarket, a bountiful selection of
nutritious nuts growing on trees.

North American trees provide a rich source of seeds for tree
squirrels. Both hardwood (deciduous) and softwood (conifers) trees generate food for squirrels. From hardwood trees
come nuts — acorns, hickories, pecans, etc. — and from
softwood trees come pine cones.

Nut-bearing trees in North America follow an erratic cycle
of production. On the average, several years out of five, large
quantities of nuts will be produced. These years are referred
to as "mast years." Most or all of the same species of trees in
a forest or orchard may experience this cycle at the same time
in an apparently synchronized pattern. Individual trees can
also follow erratic patterns of production different from
neighboring trees. Thought to have developed because of the
demand for their produce by squirrels and other animals, the
trees have gradually evolved this inconsistent growing pattern. If trees produced the same harvest every year, the natural population of animals feeding on the seeds would not stop

NUT MENU

HAZELNUT

PIGNUT
HICKORY

SHAGBARK
HICKORY

BUCKEYE

CHESTNUT

BEECHNUT

BUTTERNUT
HICKORY

PECAN

BLACK
WALNUT

NUT FACTS

NAME SPECIES NATIVE TO NORTH AMERICA	RANGE	DESCRIPTION	HARVEST	SQUIRRELS
hickory 18 species	eastern, midwestern and southern states	spherical to oblong; 3/4-1 3/4" (20-45 mm) diameter; husk in 4 sections	September to December (peak crops at 1-5 year intervals)	fox, eastern, gray, red, flying squirrels
walnut 17 species (walnuts are members of the hickory family)	states east of Mississippi River (not incl. N.E.) some western states	spherical; 1-2" (25-50 mm) diameter; kernel in 2 sections	September to December (peak crops at 1-5 year intervals)	fox, eastern gray, western gray, Ariz. gray, red, Douglas, flying squirrels
pecan 1 species (the pecan is a member of the hickory family)	southern states and southern part of midwest	oblong; 1/4-1" (6-25 mm) diameter; husk in 4 sections; kernel in 2 sections	August to October (peak crops alternate years)	fox, eastern, gray, southern flying squirrel
hazelnut (filbert) 2 species	North America	oblong; 1/2-3/4" (15-20 mm) diameter; kernel in single section	August to October (peak crops at 2-3 year intervals)	all
chestnut 1 species	states east of Mississippi River	oblong; 3/4-1 3/8" (20-35 mm); 1-3 nuts enclosed in bur	August to October	fox, eastern, gray, red, flying squirrels
beechnut 1 species	eastern states	spherical to oblong; 1/2-3/4" (12-20 mm) diameter; husk in 4 sections; 2-3 kernels per nut	September to November (peak crops at 2-20 year intervals)	fox, eastern, gray, red, flying squirrels

increasing in response; erratic annual production protects the trees' ability to reproduce.

PINE CONE CYCLES

- ponderosa pines — 3-5 year cycles of heavy cone production.
- Douglas fir — 5 year cycle of heavy cone production
- blue spruce — heavy cone production 2 out of 3 years
- Engelmann spruce — heavy cone production 2 out of 3 years

NUT TREE CYCLES

- oak — heavy acorn production 1 out of 5 years
- pecan — heavy nut production alternate years
- hickory, walnut — heavy nut production 3 out of 5 years

This cycle can be initially triggered by the effects of weather and climate. Early or late freezes, long and harsh winters, droughts, and floods all can have an effect on the production of blossoms and seeds. A late freeze, for example, may kill most or all of the buds on oak trees in a region, sharply reducing the production of acorns. With some hardwood trees, an early or late freeze may also affect seed production the following year.

Pecans, a member of the hickory family, are most affected by the heavy oil content of their nut production. Because of the heavy stress this places on the tree, a heavy-production year usually requires a low-production year following, in order for the tree to recover.

In response to these production cycles, the hoarding behavior of some squirrels — notably the red and gray squirrels — may have evolved to protect against the erratic production of nuts and cones. Some squirrel observers believe that red squirrels may survive for as long as two years on stored hoards. A red squirrel's hidden larder may contain up to 14,000 pine cones, dried mushrooms, and other foodstuffs. Typically, however, squirrels only rely on their food stores from one growing season until the next.

Squirrels and pine trees have been evolving together for thousands of years. As one changes in reaction to the other, in turn the change breeds

SEROTINOUS PINE CONE

further change. The seeds of the pine cone are one focus of this battle, a struggle for survival that benefits both sides only as long as neither side wins. The pine cone, for example, is the favorite food of the red squirrel. Buried within the red squirrel midden may be dozens of bushels of cones, stashed for uncaching in lean winter months. The caching technique of the red squirrel involves burying cones deep within the pile of litter that forms the midden, an environment that is dark, damp, and low in oxygen, keeping the cones from germinat-

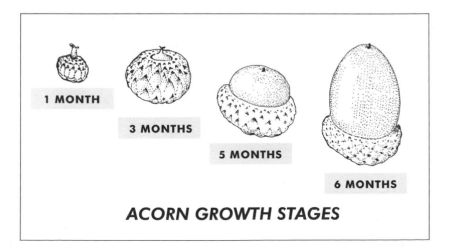

1 MONTH

3 MONTHS

5 MONTHS

6 MONTHS

ACORN GROWTH STAGES

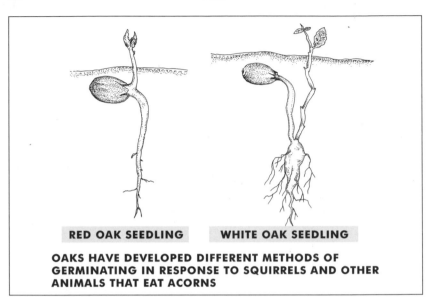

RED OAK SEEDLING   **WHITE OAK SEEDLING**

**OAKS HAVE DEVELOPED DIFFERENT METHODS OF
GERMINATING IN RESPONSE TO SQUIRRELS AND OTHER
ANIMALS THAT EAT ACORNS**

ing. This works well for the squirrel, preserving the nutritional quality of the cones. But it keeps the seeds from performing their vital function for the tree, reproduction. A study of the whitebark pine (*Pinus albicaulis*), for example, showed that up to 99 percent of the seeds produced by a tree were taken by red squirrels and birds for either eating or caching.

In response to this lack of reproductive success, one pine tree, the lodgepole pine, has developed a unique system to combat the squirrels' habits. The serotinous race of lodgepole pine produces a different kind of cone, one that is continuously being produced throughout the year. Not only does this reduce the need for the squirrel to hoard cones for the off-season, the cones are also more difficult for the squirrel to eat. The cones of the serotinous race are hard, thorny, and small. Squirrels are forced to work harder to remove them from the tree and remove the seeds from the cone. Thus, squirrels may be given a greater payback by choosing other

FAVORITE FOODS

RED SQUIRREL tree sap (maple, birch), seeds, nuts, flowers, buds, bark, berries, lichen, carrion, insects, snails, birds' eggs, nestling birds, fungi

EASTERN GRAY SQUIRREL acorns, hickory nuts, buds, twigs, seeds, insects, nestling birds

WESTERN GRAY SQUIRREL acorns, pine cones, buds, flowers, fungi, birds' eggs, nestling birds

FOX SQUIRREL tree sap, inner tree bark (maple, elm), buds, twigs, osage orange, fungi, nuts, seeds, acorns, field and sweet corn

DOUGLAS SQUIRREL pine cones, nuts, seeds, berries, grapes, fungi

NORTHERN FLYING SQUIRREL nuts, seeds, berries, buds, fungi, carrion, insects, lichens, seeds, flowers, fruits, truffles, tree sap (maple)

SOUTHERN FLYING SQUIRREL nuts, seeds, berries, buds, fungi, carrion, insects

ABERT'S SQUIRREL pine cones (predominately from ponderosa pine), pinyon seeds, nuts, berries, inner bark (cambrium), twigs, buds, flowers, pollen, fungi, carrion

types of trees for their dining and subsequently, allow the lodgepole pine a better chance of reproducing itself.

Red squirrels have also changed in response to this evolution in the lodgepole pine. Physiologically, their jaw strength has increased in response to the difficulty in eating these cones. And behaviorally, they have developed stronger territorial instincts, protecting "their" trees from other squirrels.

TREE ANATOMY

BAST FIBERS   CAMBRIUM   ANNUAL RINGS

BARK   XYLEM   PITH

Nuts such as the walnut have also evolved in tune with the habits of squirrels. In Europe, where the native squirrels are smaller than on the American continent, the walnuts have thinner shells.

Oak trees and the acorns they produce are a major food source for many animals, including squirrels. Changes in the way acorns are produced have probably occurred over time to thwart this threat. Both live oaks and white oaks, for example, have evolved a unique "rapid-response" germination. Both species have acorns that ripen, fall, and sprout in the fall months. Soon after the acorns fall to the ground — or are buried by squirrels — the seeds

The Douglas Squirrel has a distinctive eating habit. It usually eats pine cones from the bottom end up. Partially eaten cones can indicate the presence of these squirrels if they have been attacked from the bottom first. If, instead, the cone has been eaten from the top down, it is more likely to have been a crossbill finch that has been doing the dining.

FOOD TREES

Trees and shrubs providing food for squirrels include the following. Entries marked with a * indicate primary food sources. Sources vary by species and part of the country.

apple	hawthorn
arbor vitae	hazelnut
ash	hemlock*
basswood	hickory*
beech*	hornbeam
birch	huckleberry
bittersweet	incense cedar
black locust	kinnikinnick
black walnut*	maple*
blackberry	mockernut
blackgum	mountain ash
blueberry	mulberry
buckeye	oak*
butternut	osage-orange
cherry	pear
chestnut	pecan
cranberry	pine*
currants	raspberry
dogwood	salal
douglas fir*	sedge
elderberry	serviceberry*
elm*	spruce*
fir*	sweetgum
flowering dogwood	sycamore
grape	tulip tree

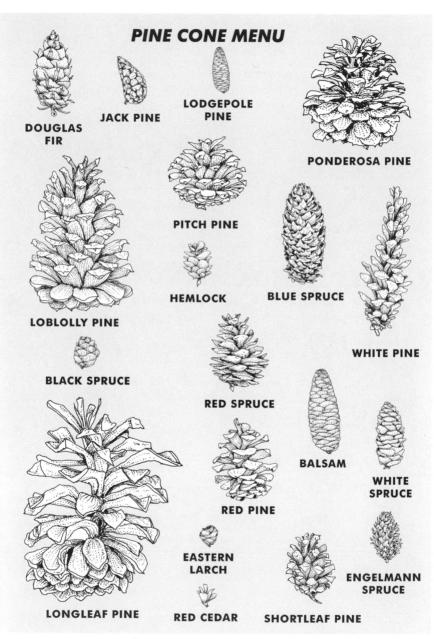

PINE CONE MENU

DOUGLAS FIR

JACK PINE

LODGEPOLE PINE

PONDEROSA PINE

PITCH PINE

LOBLOLLY PINE

HEMLOCK

BLUE SPRUCE

WHITE PINE

BLACK SPRUCE

RED SPRUCE

BALSAM

WHITE SPRUCE

RED PINE

LONGLEAF PINE

EASTERN LARCH

RED CEDAR

SHORTLEAF PINE

ENGELMANN SPRUCE

develop a root and sprout that can survive if separated from the nut. But scientists studying how gray squirrels harvest and store acorns have discovered that they often gnaw a small notch in the acorn before burying it. This notch effectively

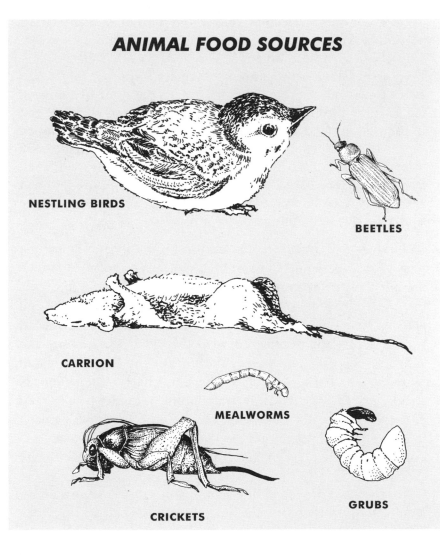

ANIMAL FOOD SOURCES

NESTLING BIRDS

BEETLES

CARRION

MEALWORMS

CRICKETS

GRUBS

degerminates the acorn, preventing it from sprouting and thus depriving the squirrel of its full nutritional content.

Black oaks, on the other hand, have acorns which ripen and fall in the autumn, but do not sprout until spring. Gray squirrels have not been observed notching acorns from black oaks. Their operations on live oak and white oak acorns have been observed in several states, including Florida, New Jersey, Illinois, and Michigan.

Squirrels have a reputation as greedy — devouring whatever is in front of them. This may describe their behavior at the average bird feeder, but in the wild they are picky eaters. In the rush to find and store nuts, they use highly developed senses to sort the good nuts from the bad. Nuts that have been infested with parasites such as worms are not stored. They may be discarded or eaten on the spot, a meal of both nutmeat and insect. The detection of these infested nuts is through the squirrel's sense of smell.

The seeds of trees are the major food for tree squirrels. Squirrel teeth and squirrel behavior have evolved to make the most of this resource. Gnawing activity is used to pierce the shells of nuts such as hazelnuts, walnuts, acorns, and pecans. Pine cones are handled with some skill; experienced squirrels rarely get smeared with the sticky resin from the cones. Tree bark is also a regular part of the larder provided by trees. The bark, or actually the inner bark (*cambrium*), is a delicacy for several other mammals, including bears and porcupines, but it is squirrels who may do the most damage to a tree in their search for this material. Stripping away the outer protective layer of bark, the exposed inner surfaces may succumb to infestations of insects or disease.

Another byproduct of the cambrium is tree sap, a target meal for squirrels particularly in the winter and spring when other food supplies may be scarce. Sap flows started by birds

FUNGI MENU

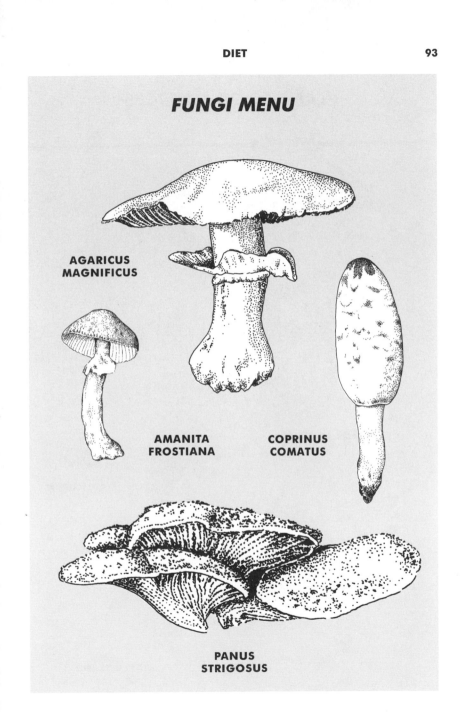

AGARICUS
MAGNIFICUS

AMANITA
FROSTIANA

COPRINUS
COMATUS

PANUS
STRIGOSUS

PLANT FOOD SOURCES

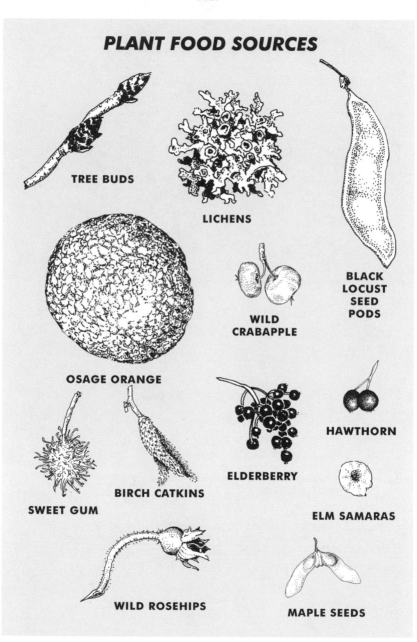

TREE BUDS

LICHENS

BLACK LOCUST SEED PODS

WILD CRABAPPLE

OSAGE ORANGE

SWEET GUM

BIRCH CATKINS

ELDERBERRY

HAWTHORN

ELM SAMARAS

WILD ROSEHIPS

MAPLE SEEDS

such as woodpeckers are often the source of this treat. Maple sugar collection in the northeast has also been known to attract squirrels to sugar taps and collection buckets. It is not unusual for northern flying squirrels to drown in these containers, the victims of their own appetite.

Although tree squirrels typically concentrate on food generated by trees — nuts, seeds, berries, twigs, etc. — they can also pursue a more varied diet. Sources of meat, including insects, carrion (rotting meat), birds' eggs, and even nestling birds are part of their food supply at different times of the year. Mushrooms are also sometimes consumed. Red squirrels have even been reported as caching these fungi by impaling them on branches or wedging them into cracks for later consumption. The northern flying squirrel is known to regularly seek out truffles growing in the ground in the root systems of oak trees.

Most tree squirrel species have also been observed occasionally gnawing on animal bones, antlers, and even turtle shells. This is probably as a source of minerals or as a control measure for their perpetually growing teeth. Pieces of bone and antler are frequently found in the food caches of squirrels.

Among the tree squirrels, the red squirrel is thought to have the strongest appetite for animal flesh. Not only does this animal eat birds' eggs and nestling birds, it has been known to frequent traps baited with meat, set out to attract other animals. Animals that are most likely to be eaten by squirrels are birds, mostly those still in the nest, birds' eggs, and insects such as butterflies, moths, caterpillars, cocoons, beetles, and ants.

Squirrels are one of the few animals known to eat fly agaric mushrooms, also known as Amanita muscaria. The Amanita has long been used by some human cultures as a source of psychedelic visions, part of religious or inebriation rituals.

NATURAL COOPERATION

In at least one case, tree squirrels and trees have established a unique beneficial partnership. Fox squirrels and longleaf pines in some areas of the south participate in a relationship that provides food for the squirrel and a growth booster for the tree. The bond forms around a type of fungi that grows in the root system of the pine. This fungi is similar in nature to truffles, a subsurface fungi usually found in conjunction with the root systems of oak trees. The pine fungi depends on the root system of the pine tree as a source of carbohydrates. As it grows, it releases plant hormones that help the tree grow, it fixes nitrogen, also helping the tree gain added sustenance from the soil, and it increases the surface through which the tree's roots can absorb water and nutrients. Squirrels find this fungi through a scent emitted by the plant and are attracted to it as a food source. Digging small, shallow holes around the base of a pine tree, they locate and remove the fungi, usually taking it somewhere else to eat. Because the spores of the fungi are indigestible, they pass through the digestive system of the squirrels and spread wherever the squirrels go, finding new pine tree root systems on which to grow.

Squirrels and chipmunks, after ingesting this mushroom, have been observed to exhibit head-twitching behavior. Another natural source of behavior alteration for squirrels is fermented tree sap or fruit which can lead to intoxication. Other plants and shrubs that are a part of the tree squirrel's diet include wild raspberry, black elderberry, red elderberry, gooseberry, bunchberry, wild strawberry, and wild rose.

Unfortunately for the squirrels, the development of agriculture added new and dangerous temptations to their natural diet. Crops planted to provide food for humans and domesticated animals also prove to be nutritious to the tree squirrel. Both native Americans and European settlers waged a constant battle with wild animals for control of their crops. Squirrels proved to be a particular menace for corn, especially when their native habitat began to be cut down or burned to make room for this crop. Plagues of squirrels attacking corn fields were a problem for farmers even before the colonies established their independence. Some colonies, counties, and municipalities responded to the threat by issuing bounties on squirrels.

Although squirrels are no longer considered a serious threat to crops, they can still be a menace for ornamental shrubbery and some types of trees in commercial operations, particularly trees such as elm and maple which are regularly attacked for their bark. Nutrition can be obtained by squirrels from this bark, but foresters and biologists believe that some bark stripping is not a result of the search for food, but a result of stress, aggression, or other behaviors.

Domesticated crops and garden plants that may be part of squirrel diets include field corn, sweet corn, wheat, soybeans, strawberries, blueberries, oats, and buckwheat.

THE NATURAL HISTORY OF PINE CONES

"Each year in midsummer they start tearing up jackpine cones for the seeds, and no Labor-Day picnic ever scattered more hulls and rinds over the landscape than they do: under each tree the remains of their annual feast lie in piles and heaps." — Aldo Leopold

Pine cones are one of the major food sources for tree squirrels. For red squirrels, Abert's squirrels, and Douglas squirrels, especially, pine cones and pine trees are a major part of the life of these animals.

The family of pine trees includes true pines (*Pinus*), spruces (*Picea*), firs (*Abies*), Douglas firs (*Pseudotsuga*), larches (*Larix*), and hemlocks (*Tsuga*). In North America, there are 61 species of pine.

Pine cones come in two varieties, male and female. Male cones carry the pollen necessary for the germination of new generations of seeds. They are characterized by their size, which is usually much smaller than female cones, and their composition, which is soft and pulpy. Female cones are the ones typically associated with the concept of pines. These cones are larger than the male and woody in composition, formed by a series of flattened scales arranged around a central stalk. Both male and female cones develop slowly, with two or more years required to produce mature cones.

Cones from several different years of development grow at the same time on the same tree. The ripened cones of the current year are attached to the tree near the juvenile buds that will form the next year's cone crop. When the pollen fertilizes the young female cones, they are small, often no more than the size of peas. As they develop, the female cones remain green and closed. Beginning with the second year, these cones gradually develop a drier, woody composition, ready for opening and release of seeds in the fall.

Until they are ripe, female pine cone scales remain tightly closed, each cone a fist. The pollen from male cones fertilizes the individual "petals" of the female cone, which nurture two seeds

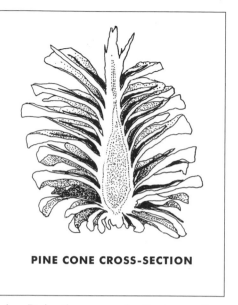

PINE CONE CROSS-SECTION

at the base of each cone scale. It is these seeds that are the edible object of the tree squirrel's quest. The female cones begin to ripen when the seeds are fertile and ready for sowing, usually in the fall months. This is when the scales dry and spread, the fist expanding into an open hand. This action exposes the seeds to an intentional fate, a scattering with the wind. Scattering is enhanced because pine cones characteristically feature thin, wing-like membranes attached to each seed, a natural sail to catch the wind.

Pine nuts are attractive targets as food for animals because of their nutritional content; they are rich in protein and calories and also contain sugar, vitamins, and other nutrients. Typically, half or more of the weight of pine nuts is fat: calories per pound may exceed 2,500, protein content can range from 15 to 30 percent. It is not surprising that squirrels and other animals are able to thrive on a diet that is mostly pine cones. Biologists have measured the calories found in various pine cones and nuts regularly eaten by squirrels and estimated the energy requirements necessary to keep a squirrel alive during winter months, a period when the animal must survive on resource caches. By these estimates, one adult red squirrel needs:

8.6 bushels of blue spruce cones

13 bushels of Douglas fir cones

24 bushels of lodgepole pine cones

Most pine cones open when ripe, exposing their seeds to the air. Because the pine nuts are rich in unsaturated oils, this action also makes them susceptible to spoiling. Oxidation is a major threat to the nutritional content of the seeds, speeding up deterioration. To combat this problem, pine cone scales

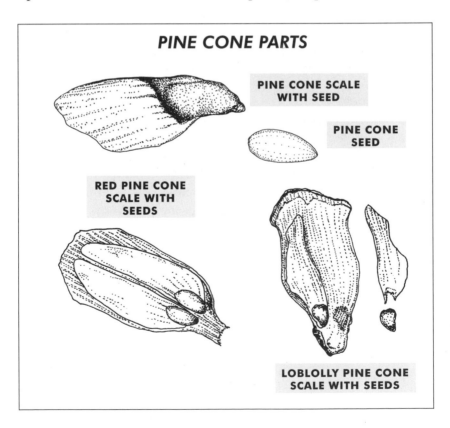

PINE CONE PARTS

PINE CONE SCALE WITH SEED

PINE CONE SEED

RED PINE CONE SCALE WITH SEEDS

LOBLOLLY PINE CONE SCALE WITH SEEDS

and pine seed coats contain natural antioxidants, compounds which help counteract the effects of exposure to oxygen. A few pines, notably the lodgepole pine, have also developed other methods for protecting their seeds against oxidation. These pines produce sessile (*serotineous*) cones, seed clusters that remain tightly closed to seal off exposure to air. Such closed cones can withstand many seasons without losing their ability to germinate. Some closed cones have been found to remain viable for up to thirty years. In this state, the cones wait for an unusual event in order to trigger opening and release of seeds. This event is fire. After a forest fire, sessile cones open quickly and help the tree take advantage of the temporary lack of competition from other trees to begin a new generation.

Squirrels have also developed the ability to take advantage of the fragile nutritional state of pine cones. In order not to lose the important nutritional content during a prolonged period when the cones may be stashed as part of a food cache, squirrels such as the red squirrel and Douglas squirrel bury cones in middens, large heaps of organic material discarded during their feeding activity. Middens are usually located in cool, shady areas and maintain a high level of moisture. Fresh cones buried in such conditions are cut off from the damaging effects of oxygen, in effect putting the seeds in a state of hibernation.

Some squirrels also routinely harvest cones before they have begun to open. These cones are stashed in the same cool, damp conditions, keeping them in great shape nutritionally until the squirrel is ready for a meal. Pine cones buried in squirrel middens may retain their nutritional qualities — and ability to germinate — for several years.

THE NATURAL HISTORY OF ACORNS

"Anyone who has watched a squirrel running over the several inches of snow, sniff here and there, then abruptly come to a halt, dig unerringly through the white mantle, leaves, and dirt and recover a buried nut cannot doubt the marvelous delicacy of their smelling powers."

— W.J. Hamilton, Jr.

Oak trees bear flowers called catkins, clusters of small blossoms. Catkins can be either male or female flowers, both found on the same tree. Pollination occurs during a one-to-two week period in the spring, with the pollen carried by the wind. Fertilized female catkins grow together in bunches, each developing a seed within a base formed by a woody cup. These seeds are what turn into the familiar acorn. Acorns reach maturity in either one or two years, depending on the species of oak.

In North America there are 59 native species of oak tree, with other types including those imported from Europe, hybrid varieties, and those growing mostly as shrubs. The two major types of oak trees are white oak — the major timber types — and red oak — distinguished by their bright red fall colors. White oaks generally produce annual crops of acorns; red oaks generally produce crops of acorns over a two-year period. Of the two, acorns from white oaks are usually sweeter. Acorns produced by red oaks contain more tannin and are bitter to the taste, although still edible.

Annual cycles of production of acorns can vary from tree to tree. Years when heavy crops are produced are referred to as mast years. At a peak, large oak trees can yield thousands

ACORN MENU

WHITE OAK

POST OAK

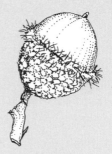

BUR OAK

OVERCUP OAK

SWAMP WHITE OAK

OREGON WHITE OAK

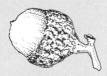

RED OAK

BLACK OAK

CHESTNUT OAK

SCARLET OAK

PIN OAK

of acorns, several hundred pounds in total weight. At an ebb, only a few hundred acorns may be developed.

Acorns yield important nutritional content for squirrels. When fresh, about half of the nut is carbohydrates, 35 percent is water, 5 percent is fat, 4 percent protein, and 4 percent crude fiber. Vitamins, minerals, trace elements, and other nutritional elements are also present. Typically, a pound of acorns is the equivalent of a little more than 1,200 calories.

SEASONAL DIET

"Tassel-eared squirrels, poker-faced but exuding emotion with voice and tail, told you insistently what you already knew full well: that never had there been so rare a day, or so rich a solitude to spend it in." — Aldo Leopold

SPRING Tree squirrels generally fare well during spring months as they are offered a wide assortment of budding greenery as food. Spring food sources include: buds on conifers and hardwood trees, staminate cones (pine cones that are produced throughout the year but remain unopened on the tree), maple samaras (the winged seeds), annual and perennial flowers, corms, bulbs, insects, fungi.

SUMMER Tree squirrels may have the least availability of food supplies during summer months, even compared to the deprivations of winter. This is because the initial abundance of spring-blooming plants is over, low moisture conditions can slow the growth of new food, and their stored food supplies may be exhausted.

FALL Beginning in late summer, ripening fruits and seeds offer squirrels their greatest opportunity to put on weight and hoard food for the winter. Pine cones begin to attract the attention of squirrels even before they have begun to open. Berries and fruits are also eaten, as are fungi. The acorn crop for the year is a major focus, usually beginning in September.

WINTER Winter months are generally spent relying on food supplies stored in the preceding months. Pine cones, nuts, and dried fungi make up the majority of this menu. Squirrels may also actively forage in winter months, depending on the weather, searching for new fungi buried under the ground, pine cones and nuts previously cached, and fresh bark.

HOARDING

*"I have a venturous fairy that shall seek the squirrels'
hoard, and fetch thee new nuts."*

— Titania, Queen of the Fairies
(A Midsummer's Night Dream, William Shakespeare)

If there is one singular characteristic that makes squirrels
unique among small mammals, it is their natural instinct to
hoard food. Actively storing food for later use adds a powerful capability to the squirrels' ability to survive. Periodic
fluctuations in the availability of food supplies as well as
changes in the number of other animals competing for available food, are forces that few animal species can overcome
unless they have such capability.

Hoarding may also have evolved in response to the cycle
of food production of the major food source for tree squirrels,
the nuts and seeds of trees. Many trees, especially conifers
and nut-bearing hardwoods, have evolved non-consistent
production cycles. In a given period of years, for example, a
tree may produce widely varying numbers of nuts from one
year to the next. Because the squirrel has caches of food, it
may be more capable of withstanding a lean year for nut
production. More likely, however, is the need for squirrels to
have a year-round supply of food while nature is taking a
break from producing fresh food, as in the winter months.
Because squirrels do not hibernate, they need this type of
resource.

Some squirrels, such as the red squirrel, have been observed using cached stores of food as late as two years after
the food was originally cached. Typically, however, squirrels
do not depend on their stores for more than the length of the
non-growing season.

Squirrels have developed sophisticated capabilities in their hoarding. Different types of food are stored in different ways to maintain quality. Mushrooms, for instance, a favorite food for most squirrels, are usually dried before storing. This is done by impaling them on small branches or leaving them in the forks of trees for later retrieval. Storage sites are then chosen for their dry conditions. Cavities in tree trunks are the most likely candidate for storage of dried mushrooms.

Pine cones, on the other hand, are often harvested while green and cached in damp conditions that keep seeds from ripening. Middens, large piles of debris that form under squirrels' regular feeding stations, are practical storage systems for pine cones because they retain moisture. Caches of pine cones buried in groups within a midden stay dormant, the moisture keeping them from drying out and opening up, prompting the internal seeds to sprout, a positive result for the pine

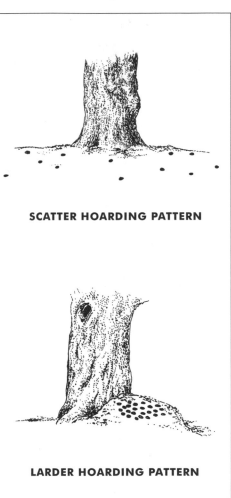

SCATTER HOARDING PATTERN

LARDER HOARDING PATTERN

SQUIRRELS USE THEIR FRONT PAWS, TEETH, AND NOSES TO BURY AND COVER THEIR HOARDS

but a negative one for the squirrel. Squirrels in the midst of green pine cone harvesting binges have been observed methodically stripping trees of their cones, often at the rate of one every few seconds.

Gray squirrels usually strip outer husks from walnuts before storing. The fibrous outer husk is soft compared to the tough inner shell, a difficult barrier even for squirrels. After burying, however, the aged shells are much easier to gnaw through.

Biologists differentiate hoarding behavior in animals into two general categories: scatter hoarding and larder hoarding. Scatter hoarding is dispersed, the storage of single nuts at separate sites. Larder hoarding, on the other hand, is characterized by the caching of a quantity of food at a single site. Tree squirrels practice both kinds of hoarding, although one species may exhibit more of one type of hoarding behavior than another.

Red squirrels have even created a combination hoarding activity. Their eating and caching behavior concentrates on one site, a location where they carry their food and consume it. The pile of debris under this site, the midden, can be extensive in size. Within the pile of debris, they bury uneaten pine cones in multiple larders of 20-30 cones each. Human pine cone hunters often seek out these middens for their easy pickings. From 2 to 15 bushels of cones have been found in a single red squirrel midden.

Food that is hoarded in scattered locations by squirrels is not easy to defend against theft by other animals, and squirrels that have scattered hoards usually do not actively defend these. On the other hand, when large caches of food are accumulated, they are often located close to the squirrels' nests and squirrels that have these hoards are often alert to and defensive against potential shrinkage of their stores.

Scatter hoarding of nuts usually provides a beneficial effect for the nuts. Squirrels typically bury individual nuts in shallow holes, from 0-2 inches (0-5.1 cm) deep. This is an ideal depth for the germination of seeds, and nuts that have not been retrieved by squirrels for eating often sprout into new trees. Individual nuts are usually buried under or close to the canopy of the tree from which they came, but squirrels regularly take nuts as far as 50 feet (15 meters) for burial.

When digging a hole to bury its food, squirrels use their front paws to scrape away soil and surface material. After the food is dropped in the resulting hole, dirt and debris is pushed into the hole with the nose and paws; sometimes a squirrel may strike the nut with its incisors to push it securely into the hole. The nose may also be used to tamp down the dirt. Scrapings of surface litter are also used to camouflage the hole site.

Once food has been dispersed and hidden, finding it again can be a problem. Not all the nuts scattered in various holes are recovered by any one squirrel; leftovers sprout into new trees, rot, or are stolen by other squirrels, birds, or small mammals. Finding hidden stores is mostly a function of smell, with results varying in response to weather conditions, moisture in the soil — drier soil yields poorer results — and the characteristic odor of the food itself. As yet unproven observations by some biologists also suggest that at least one species of squirrel, the southern flying squirrel, may secrete an oily substance with which they mark their food stores. This scent would not only aid the squirrel in locating its stores, it may function as a repellent to rival squirrels. In theory, the distinctive odor of one squirrel may be off-putting to another squirrel; they are inspired only by their own scent marks. Southern flying squirrels are, in any case, different from other American tree squirrels in that they routinely share nests, feeding areas, and territories.

Scent may not be the only way that squirrels find their hoards, however. Some studies have shown that squirrels such as the gray squirrel can use visual signs to remember where to find food. Where there are high populations of squirrels, this kind of ability could be useful because squirrels often have overlapping and shared feeding areas. At such sites, the hoards of individual squirrels may be in close proximity to each other, but grouped into distinct zones.

In one study of western fox squirrels, 99 percent of nuts that were hoarded in the fall were uncovered and eaten by the squirrels before the normal spring germination could begin. Most squirrels, however, are not thought to achieve this extreme accuracy in their hoarding. Retrieval rates are more likely to be about 50-60 percent.

Squirrels have a natural requirement to hoard food in order to survive. How they gather their food for hoarding, however, is not part of the same internal program. They take their food where they find it. Stealing from the hoards of other squirrels, for example, is a common behavior, as is raiding the caches made by birds such as blue jays. Black walnuts gathered by blue jays are frequently stolen by fox squirrels when they are stashed in the wooded areas where these squirrels normally forage. Some blue jays have been observed with an alternative storage behavior, presumably in response to this danger: they avoid losing their supplies if they place their hoards in open meadows, habitat that is avoided by fox squirrels.

Hoarding behavior is also related to necessity as much as instinct. While squirrels in general may hoard some food, how much they hoard is related to the climate. One species of squirrel will thus behave differently depending on what part of the country it is in. Southern flying squirrels are one such example, with members of this species that live in the wintry conditions of northern states shown to gather and store much more food than the members of their own species living in the more temperate conditions of the far south.

Larders cached for winter use are mostly pine cones and this kind of caching is primarily the habit of red squirrels. Nuts are less likely to be stored in such masses and gray and fox squirrels do not use larder hoarding. In areas where conifers are in abundance, squirrels are more likely to live through the winter and be less threatened by starvation. Squirrels living in hardwood forests generally have higher winter death rates. Of those that survive winter, lower body weights in the spring are more typical than for squirrels living in conifer forests.

Pine cone hoarding, however, is not consistent everywhere there are conifers. Differences in elevation and type of pine tree may make a difference in how squirrels develop and maintain their hoarding behavior. Some conifers, for example, produce pine cones throughout the year, not on a seasonal cycle. With a more regular supply at hand, squirrels in the vicinity of such trees usually do not store as many cones as squirrels in other areas.

The size of squirrel populations can depend on their hoards. Winter is a primary cause of death for tree squirrels because of starvation. In years when there are large numbers of nuts produced by trees, squirrel numbers are more likely to remain high despite the severity of the winter because there are more nuts available to be stored and eaten.

Hoarding is so critical for squirrels that it is practiced even by young squirrels. Biologists have observed active caching behavior in southern flying squirrels as early as 68 days after birth. Young fox squirrels have also been observed actively developing food hoards when only 75 days old.

Hoarding is not limited to pine cones, nuts, and fungi. Squirrels have been observed stashing berries, fruit, carrion (nestling birds, insects), and bits of antler and bone. In captivity, tame squirrels are also reported to instinctively cache some items of food, hiding them in their cages or if allowed the run of a house, depositing them in various nooks and crannies.

Most of what is known about food hoarding by tree squirrels has come from studies of the gray, red, and fox squirrels. Flying squirrels, active by night, have not provided as much information. What is known, however, shows that these unique mammals have developed a few tricks of their own. When carrying unwieldy nuts, the southern flying squirrel often notches the hull of the nut so that its incisors can grip it more securely during a glide through the air. When hiding nuts, flying squirrels rarely choose to dig in the ground like other tree squirrels. They use other sites, including behind loose bark and in small crevices in tree trunks.

SQUIRRELS IN MOTION

"Though only a few inches long, so intense is his fiery vigour and restlessness, he stirs every grove with wild life, and makes himself more important than even the huge Bears that shuffle through the tangled underbrush beneath him."   — John Muir

One of the most observable characteristics of tree squirrels is the way they move on and above the ground. As members of the rodent order, squirrels have evolved specific skeletal and muscular features to make them more efficient at what they do. They are usually clumsy, awkward runners on the surface, but are agile and at home in the environment above the ground.

Different species of tree squirrels actually have slightly different ways of moving on and above the ground. Red squirrels generally move more quickly and stay in the trees most of the time. Gray squirrels spend more time on the ground and are more likely to use the ground for escape when threatened. Fox squirrels are the fastest runners and prefer to escape from danger by staying on the ground.

Squirrels can walk or move short distances with an asymmetrical gait, different limbs moving independently. At speed, however, the natural motion of squirrels is to hop,

using both back legs together to propel themselves forward. Front legs also function together, an efficient way to cushion the impact of the body striking the ground.

Even when moving vertically, as in tree climbing, squirrels usually use their hind legs together, in effect, "hopping" up a surface. In order to move among branches and other perches that may offer little support, squirrels make use of a specialized hind foot that is similar in many ways to other mammals that live above the ground. The digits of this foot have a clasping capability, allowing the animals to grip around the diameter of a perch. Unlike mammals such as monkeys and apes, however, squirrels also have relatively large claws on all digits, giving them a useful tool for obtaining friction on rough surfaces. Because of these claws and their low body weight, squirrels are able to maneuver on vertical surfaces such as brick walls that are formidable obstacles for other climbing rodents.

In the vicinity of their nests, squirrels develop specific lanes of travel. On trunks, through the branches, and from tree to tree, they can utilize these familiar paths to escape from predators quickly.

The hind foot of tree squirrels also features another unique adaptation to its life above the ground. The joints are very flexible, allowing the legs to turn almost backward. When descending, this gives a squirrel the ability to use the claws on the hind feet as effectively as when it is climbing in the other direction.

Squirrels may be more at home in the trees, but some species are also no strangers to water. Numerous reports describe gray squirrels in particular swimming across streams, rivers, and lakes. In northern states and Canada, occasional reports have also described swimming squirrels being lunged at and eaten by large fish.

Except for the flying squirrels, which are nocturnal, tree squirrels are active during the day. Depending on the time of year, weather conditions, and species, peak activity during the day may vary, but most squirrels are most active early in the day and at the end of the day. Occasionally, squirrels may also be active into the evening hours after the sun sets. Except for brief periods during extreme winter weather conditions, squirrels are also likely to spend time every day foraging for food. During periods of extreme heat at the height of the summer, activity may slow. Even in the northern areas of their range, however, they do not hibernate.

One unique characteristic of squirrel activity is that sometimes they will be more active during periods of light rain. Some scientists believe this unusual behavior is a practical response to their food supply. Much of the year, even when fresh food is available, squirrels will seek out and eat pine cones and nuts that they have hoarded. Most of this hoarding is done in a "scatter" method, with individual items buried throughout their territory. Although there is some evidence that squirrels can locate these food stashed from visual clues, most of the recovery comes from the scent of the buried items. When the ground is damp, more scent is released and the squirrels have an easier time finding their food. Thus, rain may mean "feeding time."

FLYING SQUIRRELS

"A more gentle, docile, and graceful animal than the Flying-squirrel does not exist; and though without anything striking in the way of colour or markings, it is nevertheless one of the most beautiful of our mammals." — C. Hart Merriam

The northern and southern flying squirrels exhibit a capability for flight — or more appropriately, soaring — because of a unique fold of skin. This type of unpowered flight by animals and airplanes is sometimes referred to as *volplaning.* The squirrels' gliding capability comes from the *patagium,* a large flap of skin extending from the front leg to the rear leg, attached to the wrist and the ankle with a spur of cartilage. The squirrel can extend the flap to produce a wide, flat, surface that gives it considerable aerodynamic capability. The flap is covered with short, smooth fur that produces little drag. When sitting, the flap bunches up along the squirrel's sides and does not hinder it from moving around on the ground or in trees, but the flying squirrel is notably less agile on the ground than other tree squirrels.

In flight, the squirrel can maneuver from side to side by moving alternate limbs or using its tail like a rudder. Flight distances are controlled by stalling, using an upward movement of the flaps to slow and shorten the glide path.

Most jumps by flying squirrels are short, from 30 to 50 feet, but they are capable of glides of up to 150 feet. There are reports of individual glides that have exceeded 200 feet. During a glide, squirrels are capable of multiple, sharp turns of up to 90 degrees to avoid limbs or other obstructions.

Flights by flying squirrels are normally at an angle between 30 and 50 degrees, the optimum position for aerodynamic lift according to their shape and body mass.

Flights are initiated from a head-down position. Distances and landing points are gauged before launching; squirrels can be seen moving their head rapidly up and down and from side to side in order to gain more visual information before they jump. Just after the squirrel launches itself into the air, the body becomes almost horizontal, the limbs extended to stretch the skin flaps. As the flight nears its destination, the squirrel uses the flaps as air brakes, developing more air resistance to slow its descent by raising the front part of its body. Because the landing zone is most likely to be a vertical surface — the trunk of a tree — the position will become almost vertical, allowing the squirrel to cushion its landing with a simultaneous touchdown with all four paws. In fact, flying squirrels usually avoid soaring unless they can land on a vertical surface. The flights are soundless but a soft thump may indicate a successful landing.

Young flying squirrels first venture out of their nests about five weeks after they are born. Also within 5-6 weeks, they may take their first exploratory flights, action that is instinctive and not taught by the mother squirrel.

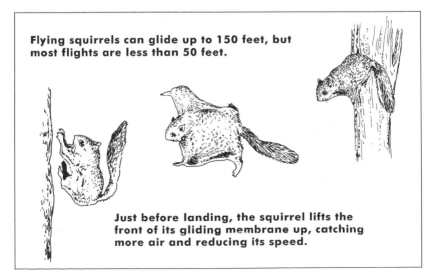

Flying squirrels can glide up to 150 feet, but most flights are less than 50 feet.

Just before landing, the squirrel lifts the front of its gliding membrane up, catching more air and reducing its speed.

NESTS

"All squirrels depend, for permanent dens, on a delicately balanced equilibrium between a rotting cavity and the scar tissue with which the tree attempts to close the wound. The squirrels referee the contest by gnawing out the scar tissue when it begins unduly to shrink the amplitude of their front door." — Aldo Leopold

Nest types vary among the squirrel species. Different materials and building styles may offer some observational clues about what type of squirrel may be in the area. Leaf nests are traditionally called *dreys*. In cold climates or in fall and winter months most tree squirrels will switch from outside nests to inside quarters, usually tree cavities formed by rot, insects, or woodpeckers.

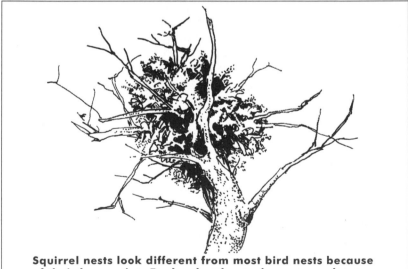

Squirrel nests look different from most bird nests because of their larger size. Eagles, hawks, and crows may have nests that are as large, but these are flattened and open at the top.

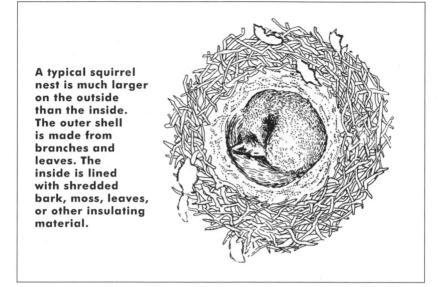

A typical squirrel nest is much larger on the outside than the inside. The outer shell is made from branches and leaves. The inside is lined with shredded bark, moss, leaves, or other insulating material.

Squirrels generally keep their nests clean, periodically building new nests and moving in order to limit the problem with pests such as fleas. Food and body wastes are not present in the nests of most squirrels, but flying squirrels are an exception. These small mammals maintain a corner of their nests as a latrine. But even the cleanest nests could hardly be considered sanitary; they are home to a host of parasitic and pest insects that look upon the host as a source of food. One study of squirrel nests in England found the presence of specialized beetles that seek out such quarters due to the presence of fleas, a primary food source for the beetles. One of these beetle species, *Dendrophilus punctatus*, is also frequently present in bird nests, ant nests, and near sources of rotting wood or carrion.

Most tree squirrels have more than one nest in active use. Periodically switching between nests and adding new nest sites has practical consequences for the squirrels. Changing nests helps keep parasites under control, it provides more

NEST VARIETIES

EASTERN GRAY SQUIRREL   Irregular shaped nest placed in outer branches, constructed of leaves and small branches with leaves attached, shredded bark, or moss. Diameter: 15-20 inches wide, about 12 inches high. Height above ground: 25-60 feet. One entrance. May use tree cavities during cold weather.

WESTERN GRAY SQUIRREL   Large bulky nests are placed high in trees, constructed of leaves and small branches with leaves attached, shredded bark, or moss. Uses live oak, madrone, and conifers. Diameter: 18-24 inches. Height above ground: 25-60 feet. One entrance. May use tree cavities.

RED SQUIRREL   Spherical nests placed high in branches, constructed of small branches, twigs with leaves removed, bark, grass, or moss. Diameter: about 12 inches. One entrance. May use tree cavities, especially during cold weather. Also known to use ground cavities.

FOX SQUIRREL   Large spherical nest placed in outer branches, constructed of small branches, twigs, small branches with leaves attached, grass, pine needles, or moss. Nests larger than those of gray squirrel. Diameter: 15-24 inches wide. One entrance. Nests most common during warm months; uses tree cavities during cold weather. Warm weather dreys may also include smaller units and open platforms used for resting and eating.

FLYING SQUIRREL   Small nests close to trunk, constructed of leaves and shredded bark. Prefers tree cavities with narrow entrance holes, 1-2 inches in diameter.

ABERT'S SQUIRREL   Large bulky nests high in conifer tree forks or branches, constructed of small pine branches and twigs. Diameter: 15-24 inches. Height above ground: 40-60 feet. Two or three entrances. May use tree cavities, especially in cold weather.

DOUGLAS SQUIRREL   Irregular nests are usually in conifers, constructed of small branches and pine twigs. Diameter: 15-20 inches. Height above ground: 15-60 feet. One entrance. Prefers tree cavities.

opportunities to escape from predators, and it provides closer access to feeding sites. The number of active nests per squirrel varies, but the average is thought to be about three, with the potential to have double this number not in active use at the same time. Squirrels have been observed with as many as ten nests constructed in one year. The number can change depending on the season, the density of the squirrel population, and the availability of food.

Squirrels that use nest cavities usually adapt existing holes. Their chisel-like front teeth are well-suited to expanding entrances and excavating woody material. Nest cavities are lined with soft organic material that helps insulate from the cold. Such material is usually gathered from nearby sources and includes tree bark, twigs, leaves, mosses, lichens, animal fur and hair, bird feathers, and the contents of other nests, including those of birds and other squirrels.

External nests are usually built from scratch. Juvenile squirrels are sometimes seen practicing nest building before they have left their first homes. Squirrels build nests from materials locally available; one species will favor the same materials throughout its range.

Nest building is rarely a complicated or lengthy process. Most squirrels construct their nests within a day, although additional material may be added over time, before birthing, or with a change in weather. Some squirrels assemble a nest, that is, they loosely weave together a roughly spherical structure that is hollow in the center. Most often, however, the process involves little more than the construction of materials roughly laced together. When the mass reaches the desired diameter, the squirrel forces its head and body into the center, pushing the woven material out and widening a cavity large enough for comfort, a diameter of 6 to 8 inches is usually enough. Additional lining material is then added for insulation.

TERRITORY

"Though unacquainted with the first principle of sanitation, the species has developed some of the fundamentals of government. It will fight bravely for its food-tree, for its territory, for its nest ..." — Ernest Thompson Seton

Territory and its defense defines a significant part of the behavior of the red squirrel, but is of little importance to gray and fox squirrels. Aggressively defending their territory year-round, red squirrels will challenge and chase intruding squirrels, including larger species such as the gray squirrel. The other squirrels are less driven by this instinct, and might even be considered social animals, at least in some respects.

Gray and fox squirrels, except when the females are breeding and raising young, coexist without apparent conflict. Several squirrels may even occupy the same nest and exhibit mutual grooming activity. During the winter season, this shared nesting is more likely, but it has been observed throughout the year. Even in urban locations, gray and fox squirrels may have shared nesting sites, particularly where there is a scarcity of suitable nests or an artificial abundance of food. The frequent contact that such shared living quarters brings has a down side — the spread of disease and parasites, particularly the mange mite.

Flying squirrels may take nest sharing to an extreme. Dozens of these small mammals have been found in the same nest cavities, although this behavior is more frequent in the winter when cold temperatures make such sharing beneficial.

Squirrels may follow regular patterns of checking and marking the boundaries of selected areas, defined by specific sources of food such as nut trees. This continual updating serves less to maintain their own security than to allow a quick response if new food resources become available.

When more than one squirrel uses a specific tree for feeding, each squirrel may use a seperate area for its stash. This

HOME TURF

ABERT'S SQUIRREL Solitary. Density may vary from 0.04 to 0.45 squirrels per acre (0.1 to 1.1 squirrels per hectare).

FOX SQUIRREL Mostly solitary. Density may vary from 0.4 to 2.83 squirrels per acre (1 to 7 squirrels per hectare). Fox squirrels in the wild and in urban areas may be somewhat social, feeding and nesting in small groups.

EASTERN GRAY SQUIRREL Mostly solitary. Natural minimum: 1 1/2 acres per squirrel in nonurban areas. Can range up to 5 miles from nest. Density may vary from 0.4 to 6.5 squirrels per acre (1 to 16 squirrels per hectare). High population density in the wild or in urban areas and parks may prompt shared feeding areas and nests.

WESTERN GRAY SQUIRREL Solitary.

ARIZONA GRAY SQUIRREL Solitary.

RED SQUIRREL Solitary. Rarely ranges more than 250 yards from nest. Density may vary from 0.12 to 2 squirrels per acre (0.3 to 5 squirrels per hectare).

DOUGLAS SQUIRREL Density may vary from 0.12 to 0.81 squirrels per acre (0.3 to 2 squirrels per hectare).

SOUTHERN FLYING SQUIRREL Often found in pairs. Density may vary from 1 to 5 squirrels per acre (3 to 12 squirrels per hectare). Particularly in the winter, large groups of flying squirrels may share nests.

NORTHERN FLYING SQUIRREL Often found in pairs. Density may vary from 0.4 to 0.8 squirrels per acre (1 to 2 squirrels per hectare). Particularly in the winter, large groups of flying squirrels may share nests.

behavior minimizes the conflict over food and permits more squirrels to take advantage of the same resource.

Populations of squirrels fluctuate in size like many mammals, dependent on cycles of food availability, climate, disease, and other factors. Except in urban areas where artificial supplies of food and a scarcity of predators are the norm, there is no standard number of squirrels that can be expected in any part of the country.

Because of their ability to reproduce rapidly and the fact that sometimes squirrels will migrate from one area to another, the number of squirrels seen in any one area may change dramatically from one year to the next. Populations in the wild have been reported as increasing or decreasing by a factor of ten in the course of a year.

REPRODUCTION

"...wild, free Gray-squirrels do not pair, except for a day and a night, or at most two days and two nights, until the female is satisfied and the male exhausted and glad to go away and rest up for the next mate that he can find."

— Vernon Bailey

Tree squirrels may limit their own reproduction in periods when there is little food. Although it is unknown how this may be accomplished, observations of squirrel activity confirm that few or no litters of young squirrels are a characteristic of the breeding season following a year of scarcity in local food supplies. In years when squirrels in a particular region have more than one litter, the second mating period coincides with the beginning of the season when a bumper crop of pine cones is just beginning to ripen. Thus, squirrel populations are able to quickly respond to appropriate conditions and expand in size, quickly making up for the loss of life brought about by a previous scarcity of food.

Litter numbers also vary consistently as a function of geography, southern states being warmer and more verdant through the winter months than the northern states, for example. In extremely favorable conditions — good weather and abundance of food — tree squirrels are most likely to have multiple mating seasons and litters in the same year. Even squirrels found in geographic extremes in the northern latitudes where winters are long, may occasionally be inspired to have multiple litters in a single year if conditions are sufficiently encouraging.

The squirrels in a given population may not respond to the same conditions in the same way, however. The percentage of adult female squirrels with multiple litters in a given year is not 100 percent. With normal conditions in regions where multiple litters are common, less than half of the females may actually have multiple litters in one year. Younger females, especially those in their first year of sexual maturity, are the most likely to have a single litter.

Females of most squirrel species come into estrus — a specific period of fertility common to some mammals — around the first of the year, probably triggered by the gradual lengthening of the daylight period following the winter solstice in late December. Tassel-eared squirrels have a later breeding period, usually in late spring.

Female squirrels attract mates through scent, a particular scent pattern indicates that they have come into estrus and are fertile. At the time of estrus, male squirrels will abandon their normal territorial boundaries to pursue the attentions of a female. Males fight each other usually without physical harm — more threat and bluff than action — to determine dominance, a factor based mostly on maturity. It is not simply that the largest squirrel wins; it is the eldest. The prize is the right to mate with the female. And once this dominance has been established, neighboring squirrels remember who is boss.

Breeding activity varies somewhat among the tree squirrel species, but generally involves one or more males pursuing a single female. Mating chases are common, with the males chasing after a female until she is ready to accept one. It is possible the mating chase may even be essential for fertility; the chase triggering ovulation.

Females may mate with more than one male and often mate more than one time. Female squirrels are only receptive to mating for a short period, one or two days. Gray squirrels, however, may continue to attract mates for several weeks, cycling in and out of a receptive state, if they are not quickly impregnated.

Squirrels can have litters sired by more than one male, but a single male typically does the fathering for a single litter. After mating — an act usually lasting less than a minute but may take longer — a unique physical process takes place. The male squirrel emits a waxy substance after ejaculating, producing a plug in the vagina that prevents any sperm from other males from reaching the fertile eggs.

Male fox and gray squirrels have a *baculum*, a bone in the penis. This bone is about 1 centimeter in length; the baculum is almost nonexistent in red squirrels. The penis of the red squirrel is distinctively different than the other species of squirrels, lacking a prominent bone and being very long, thin, and flexible. Correspondingly, female red squirrels have a unique coiled vagina that is adapted for this appendage.

Gestation periods for squirrels vary with the general body size of the species. The large squirrels such as the gray squirrel, fox squirrel and the Abert's squirrel have gestation periods of 38-46 days; the smaller squirrels such as the red

Baby squirrels are born hairless and with their eyes and ears closed.

At five weeks, young squirrels have grown a coat of fur and can actively explore their nests.

A squirrel baby is carried with its body carefully gripped in the mother's mouth.

squirrel and the flying squirrel usually have gestation periods of less than 38 days.

Squirrels usually have between 1 and 5 young in a litter. Average litter sizes range from 2 to 4, with evidence that litters are usually larger the farther north in the squirrel's range. Squirrel litters have been reported with up to 9 young.

Baby squirrels are born blind, hairless, and with their ear flaps closed. From birth, however, they do have whiskers and claws. The infants are tiny. Flying squirrels weigh about 1/4 ounce (6 gms) each at one extreme and fox squirrels weigh about 2/3 ounces (18 gms) each at the other. Fur begins to grow at 1-2 weeks; eyes and ear flaps begin opening within 4-5 weeks. Squirrel milk, like in many small mammals, is a rich source of nutrients that promotes rapid growth. Baby squirrels, however, are nurtured for a longer period than other rodents. Weaning is at 8-10 weeks (6-9 weeks for flying squirrels).

Mother squirrels are attentive, protective parents. In times of stress or when threatened, they may move the young to a new nesting location. When moving their young, they use a distinctive method of carrying their babies, the mother gripping the baby's belly with its mouth, the head and rear feet of the baby curled around the side of the mother's head.

Both male and female squirrels are capable of reproducing at 10-12 months. Females often have their first litters the year after they are born.

The teats of female squirrels are flesh-colored until their first pregnancies, after which they turn a darker color permanently. The scrotum of male squirrels also becomes darker in color when the squirrels become sexually mature. Adult male fox and gray squirrels may occasionally have retracted testicles outside of the mating season, an occurrence that has caused some observers to conclude that such squirrels have been emasculated. One myth about squirrels, in fact, is that red squirrels, the most aggressive of the tree squirrels, are guilty of fighting with these larger species and biting off their testicles. Some early naturalists helped perpetuate this myth by reporting it as a scientific fact, but it is not true.

SQUIRREL SIGNS

"Go where you will, throughout the noble woods of the Sierra Nevada, among the giant pines and spruces of the lower zones, up through the towering silver firs to the storm-bent thickets of the summit peaks, you everywhere find this little Squirrel the master-existence."

— John Muir

Nature watchers can take advantage of the activities and habits of tree squirrels, discovering their presence in cities, backyards, parks, or woods. Squirrels, like most animals, leave telltale signs behind them that can tell the knowledgeable observer what the squirrel was doing and often, what species of squirrel was present.

FOOD DEBRIS

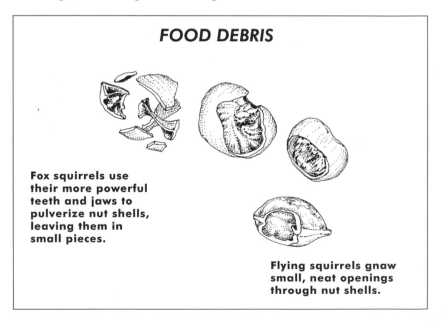

Fox squirrels use their more powerful teeth and jaws to pulverize nut shells, leaving them in small pieces.

Flying squirrels gnaw small, neat openings through nut shells.

TRACKS

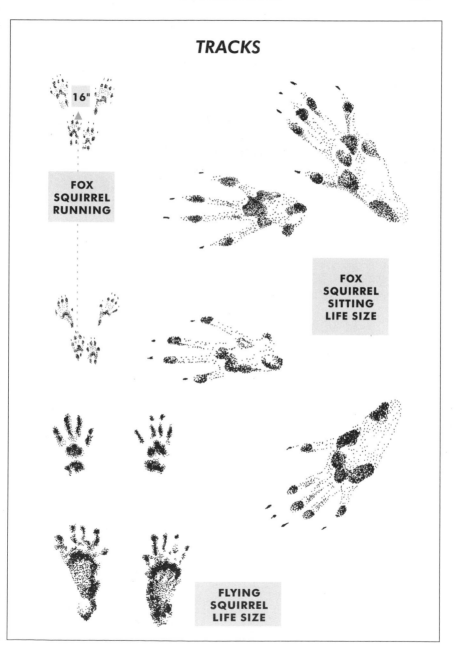

16"

FOX SQUIRREL RUNNING

FOX SQUIRREL SITTING LIFE SIZE

FLYING SQUIRREL LIFE SIZE

SCAT

Mammal droppings are referred to as scat and can be useful for identification. Squirrel scat is found as small pellets, usually located near nests and feeding sites.

FOX SQUIRREL

RED SQUIRREL

GRAY SQUIRREL

FLYING SQUIRREL

BARK MARKS

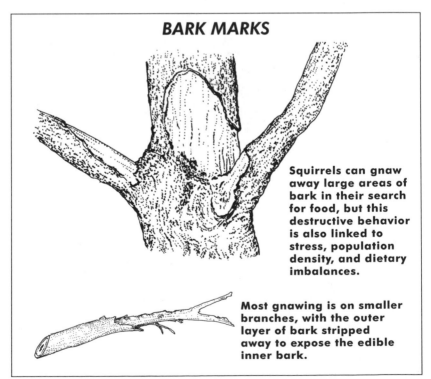

Squirrels can gnaw away large areas of bark in their search for food, but this destructive behavior is also linked to stress, population density, and dietary imbalances.

Most gnawing is on smaller branches, with the outer layer of bark stripped away to expose the edible inner bark.

SQUIRREL SOUNDS

Like most mammals that are vocal, tree squirrels use their voices to communicate. The range of communications may include warnings to other squirrels intruding in their territory, mating calls, alarm calls to warn of predators, scolding calls aimed at juveniles, and screams if injured or attacked.

ABERT'S SQUIRREL A deeper "CHUCK CHUCK CHUCK" similar to the fox squirrel.

FLYING SQUIRREL High-pitched "CHWEEP CHWEEP CHWEEP" whistles similar in tone to a bird call. Northern flying squirrels slightly lower in tone than southern flying squirrels.

FOX SQUIRREL "CHUCK CHUCK CHUCK" that is deeper and slower than the gray squirrel.

GRAY SQUIRREL Raspy "CRRK CRRK CRRK" or "QUACK, QUACK, QUACK" (similar to a duck). Eastern and western gray squirrels sound similar.

RED SQUIRREL High-pitched "TCHK TCHK TCHK" or chatter. Red squirrels were originally named "chickarees" because of their distinctive vocal calls.

DOUGLAS SQUIRREL High-pitched "TCHK TCHK" similar to red squirrel, but often in two-note pairs.

NOTE: Recordings of squirrel voices can be found on the CD-ROM, *Multimedia Audubon's Mammals* (Creative Multimedia Corporation, Portland, OR, 503-241-4351). This 2-disc set also includes reproductions of all of the birds and mammals — including squirrels — illustrated by John James Audubon from his original books.

MIGRATION

"Onward they come, devouring on their way every thing that is suited to their taste, laying waste the corn and wheat-fields of the farmer; and as their numbers are thinned by the gun, the dog, and the club, others fall in and fill up the ranks, till they occasion infinite mischief, and call forth more than empty threats of vengeance."
— John James Audubon

Squirrels are not considered to be a migratory animal. Living conditions in local areas, however, can place pressure on local populations and force many of these animals to seek out new territory. Not a true migration, this is a permanent change of address. Gray squirrels are traditionally the culprits in these movements, usually the result of a dearth of food, most often the result of the natural variations in production of nuts or pine cones. Hundreds or thousands of squirrels can be on the move at the same time in one of these unique mobilizations.

John James Audubon was convinced that the gray squirrel was actually a distinct species because of this habit. His original scientific name for the gray was *Sciurus migratorius* (migratory squirrel). Historical records of large numbers of squirrels moving through areas are found for 1749 (Pennsylvania), 1808 (Ohio), 1842 (Wisconsin), and the 1930s (Connecticut). During the 1749 episode in Pennsylvania, historical records indicate that 640,000 were killed. This record exists because gray squirrels were considered such a menace to agricultural crops that the state offered a bounty of three pence (pennies) per dead squirrel in order to encourage their control.

One of the most recent mass movements of gray squirrels occurred in 1968. Throughout the southern region of the

"When squirrels are on a journey, and their course is interrupted by a river, they all return to the next forest, as if by mutual consent, and provide themselves with a piece of the bark of a tree, with which they return to the river, and launching their little boat, jump on it with great agility, when, erecting their broad tail like a sail, they are wafted by the wind to the opposite shore. In this manner they often cross lakes of several miles in breadth, and if the weather is calm and fine, have a pleasant and prosperous journey; but it often happens that a little gust of wind oversets the whole fleet, and consigns the little, hardy adventurers to the watery grave. When such a catastrophe happens, the Laplanders consider it as a most fortunate event; and collect the little bodies as they are washed on shore, the flesh of which they eat, and sell the skins." — John Church
1824, *A Cabinet of British Quadrupeds*

Appalachian Mountains, a late frost destroyed much of the food normally produced by trees; the previous year, a maximum cycle of food production had allowed local squirrel populations to develop unusually high numbers. With too many squirrels and too little food, tens of thousands of squirrels moved in search of better conditions. This movement resulted in large numbers of squirrels crushed by cars on roadways and many squirrels were reported drowning while swimming across bodies of water.

Mass movements of squirrels in the United States have not been as frequent or as prolific in modern times as in the past.

This may be because of the elimination of much of the hard-wood forests that harbored major populations of squirrels, particularly the gray squirrel. In recent times, gray squirrels are more likely to reside in urban areas, where the horticultural practices of city dwellers provides them an ideal habitat and one less likely to become overcrowded.

When mass movements occurred in the past, they were most frequent in late summer or early fall, long before the seasonal periods when peak natural food production would occur. Reacting to clues that may include the availability of buds, flowers, developing fruit and seeds, squirrels react ahead of time to potential shortages of food in order to find new supplies before it is too late. Juvenile squirrels are also ready to seek out new territory from late summer into fall. Sometimes referred to as the "fall reshuffle," the newest generation of squirrels seeks out new sources of food such as nut trees with a ripening harvest.

In an instinctive urge to survive the upcoming seasonal dearth of food supplies, squirrels may be spurred as early as August to react to a poor crop of ripening nuts. By moving to a new area soon enough, the squirrels may be instinctively attempting to gain time on the approach of winter. If they find new food soon enough, they can store enough to survive the lean months. A delay might be deadly.

Gray squirrels were brought into Great Britain for the first time in the mid-1800s. By the 1930s, these non-native animals had become permanently established in the southern part of the country and were expanding their range. More aggressive and omnivorous than the native European red squirrel, gray squirrels have caused agricultural losses and damage to trees and buildings, but many English wildlife lovers appreciate them anyway, as they are much more likely to reside in parks and urban areas than their native cousins.

THE SQUIRREL MENACE

"Were this species to confine its depredations to the fruit of the hickory, chestnut, beech, oak and maple, it would be less obnoxious to the farmer; but unfortunately for the peace of both, it is fond of the green Indian-corn and young wheat, to which the rightful owner imagines himself to have a prior claim."

—John James Audubon, John Bachman

After all, squirrels are rodents, and have a long tradition of being a pest to humans. In previous eras, the primary damage caused by these creatures was to agricultural products, both crops ripening in the field and those in storage. Corn in particular is a favorite target of squirrels, although they rarely cause as much problem as raccoons. Some squirrels, particularly fox squirrels, have been observed building and using temporary summer nests in close proximity to fields of corn.

In more recent years, squirrels have also become the enemy of many foresters and commercial tree growers. They eat the nuts and pine cones that would otherwise develop into new trees; they strip the bark from some mature trees in a search for the nutrients of the inner layers and sweet sap; and they hungrily seek out new buds and flowers that trees produce to create seeds. The extent of this damage is difficult to estimate but is usually not the most potent threat to tree production; that award would go to insect pests. At the same time, in any case, squirrels, in performing their natural hoarding rituals, help spread new seeds throughout a forest environment.

In modern times, squirrels get into much more trouble interacting with the urban environment. Their perpetual quest to gnaw — a natural response to the never-ending growth of their unique chisel-like teeth — makes them a threat to electrical wires, siding on buildings, ornamental trees and shrubs, garden bulbs, outdoor furniture, and much more. At least when messing with electrical power transmission, the squirrels are likely to suffer the ultimate punishment, death by electrocution. The annual loss from power outages caused by squirrels is estimated to be in the millions of dollars.

Local power companies spend much of their time dealing with broken connections, shorts, and stripped insulation left behind in this chewing frenzy. Although mostly minor incidents, squirrels can get into bigger trouble. A typical example is from May 4, 1992, in the Los Angeles area. About 13,000 residences lost power for several hours after a meandering squirrel caused a short circuit at a power distribution station.

FIRST AID FOR SQUIRREL BITES

It is unlikely that a squirrel will bite a human hard or deep enough to require stitches, but infections are always a risk. Those bitten should wash the wound site and surrounding area with soap and water. It is acceptable but not necessary to further clean the wound with an antiseptic agent such as isopropyl alcohol or diluted hydrogen peroxide. Deep wounds should always be examined and cared for by appropriate medical personnel.

Tetanus shots are important for such bites. The recommendation is to get a tetanus injection or a booster shot within twenty-four hours of the biting incident if the person bitten has not had such a booster within the previous five years. Rabies may be carried by squirrels, but this is rare.

Although it is unlikely that squirrels will become a threatened species in American cities, they do pose an increasing hazard to city dwellers. Urban squirrel survival is made possible by artificially large supplies of food — natural food sources supplemented by garbage, ornamental and edible plantings, food left out for birds and pets, and food specifically offered to the squirrels themselves.

As a consequence, unnaturally large concentrations of squirrels may be found in some parks and municipal open spaces, leading to more aggressive behavior. Scattered reports indicate the nature of this problem. At Rice University in Houston, Texas, for example, about six students a year report bites from squirrels on campus.

Squirrels can carry rabies, but it is a rare disease in this mammal. In urban areas, squirrels have never been a major source of rabies contamination and are not considered a threat to public health.

SQUIRREL REPELLENT

An old-fashioned but effective deterrent to keep squirrels away from plants, attics, garden sheds, or other treasures worth preserving: **moth balls or flakes.** *Take precautions, however, to keep these chemicals from being eaten by children. Pets will leave them alone.*

BIRD FEEDERS: SQUIRREL DEFENSE

1. Locate feeders at least six to ten feet from any vertical or horizontal surface from which squirrels can jump.

2. Mount feeders by hanging from horizontal wires protected by rotating cylinders (empty film canisters, for example).

3. Mount feeders on metal or wooden poles protected by squirrel barriers. These include conical collars and metal sheathing to eliminate traction.

4. If squirrels and birds have equal access to feeders, minimize or eliminate peanuts and sunflower seeds which are especially attractive to squirrels. Peanut butter should also be eliminated from shared feeding situations — the squirrels will never leave any for the birds.

5. Use commercial bird feeders designed to thwart squirrels.

6. Add a separate feeding area for squirrels, away from bird feeding stations. Keep this area supplied with food preferred by squirrels.

FEEDING SQUIRRELS

"Every wind is fretted by his voice, almost every hole and branch feels the sting of his sharp feet. How much the growth of the trees is stimulated by this means it is not easy to learn, but his action in manipulating their seeds is more appreciable." — *John Muir*

Most urban wildlife lovers already feed squirrels if they have bird feeders, although it may be unintentionally. Squirrels are champion raiders of bird feeders and in recent years have even been responsible for the creation of a competitive new mini-industry, the design of squirrel-proof bird feeders. Most bird lovers will also be the first to admit that most of these designs don't work; squirrels have had a head start of thousands of years of evolution. Locating new food supplies and utilizing their unique athletic abilities to get to it is a major squirrel talent.

For those wildlife lovers who aim to give squirrels a food supply of their own, seed mixtures and dispensers are available for that express purpose. As bird feeder owners will attest, sunflower seeds and peanuts are at the top of the list in attracting squirrels. Although squirrels may not ignore any food type in times of need, in general they prefer larger, oilier seeds and nuts. Corn, shelled or on the cob, is also an attractive and nutritious treat. Fresh or dried, squirrels have been sharing this indigenous plant since it was first domesticated, much to the dismay of gardeners and farmers.

Fruit (apples, bananas, citrus) is also prime fodder for these rodents. Table scraps — especially processed foods, sweets, and garbage — are not appropriate for squirrels.

Bird feeders may suffer rapid wear and abuse if they are accessible to squirrels. Squirrels frequently gnaw on wood

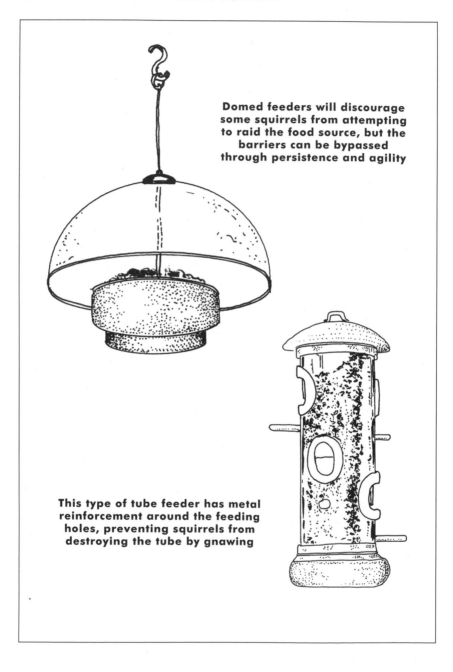

Domed feeders will discourage some squirrels from attempting to raid the food source, but the barriers can be bypassed through persistence and agility

This type of tube feeder has metal reinforcement around the feeding holes, preventing squirrels from destroying the tube by gnawing

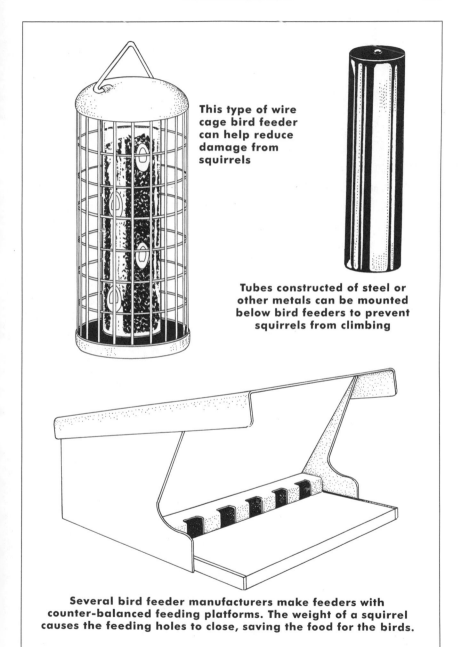

This type of wire cage bird feeder can help reduce damage from squirrels

Tubes constructed of steel or other metals can be mounted below bird feeders to prevent squirrels from climbing

Several bird feeder manufacturers make feeders with counter-balanced feeding platforms. The weight of a squirrel causes the feeding holes to close, saving the food for the birds.

WARNING

Feeding squirrels or birds from a window sill or a feeder mounted on a window can result in unwanted intrusions. If a squirrel thinks there is more food on the other side of the window, it will make a habit of coming inside to forage, making a mess of upholstery, drapes, and other furnishings. If it has entered once, a squirrel will chew through window screens to return.

and plastic parts to gain access or to enlarge openings. Smaller feeders may be completely destroyed in the process of feeding. When feeders are emptied, some squirrels appear to express their dissatisfaction with destructive, even spiteful gnawing.

The only solution satisfactory to all parties — human, birds, and squirrels — is to restrict access for the squirrel and provide separate feeding facilities. Because birds usually scatter food as they eat, the solution may be nothing more than the ground underneath the feeder.

Squirrel feeders have recently become available commercially in most parts of the country. A variety of designs are available, including models that encourage athletic antics from the squirrels for the viewing enjoyment of humans. Some models also feature hinged lids, requiring squirrels to display some learned techniques to get at the food supplies. Fans of these type of feeders have reported that some squirrels have apparently learned another use for the hinged lids: repetitive lifting and dropping when the feeders are empty to signal their benefactors to replenish the food supply.

DO-IT-YOURSELF SQUIRREL FEEDER

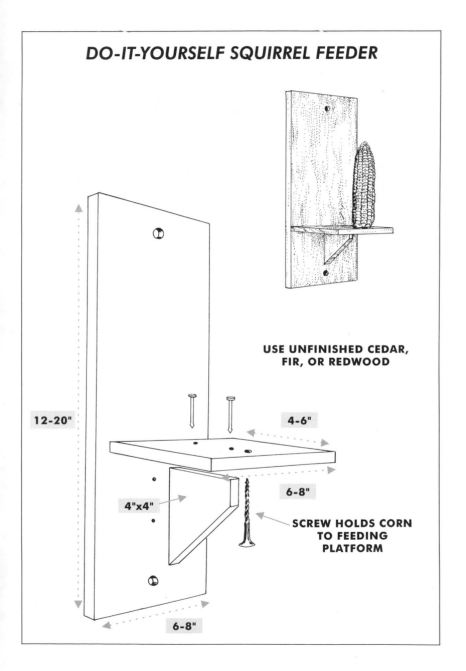

USE UNFINISHED CEDAR, FIR, OR REDWOOD

12-20"

4-6"

6-8"

4"x4"

SCREW HOLDS CORN TO FEEDING PLATFORM

6-8"

Squirrels have been known to raid hummingbird feeders for the sweet liquid inside. In the process, the delicate contraptions may be damaged by their gnawing or dropped and destroyed by the unplanned-for weight of the larger animals.

While many bird lovers may hold a grudge against squirrels for making their avocation more difficult, others have not only learned to live with these pesky creatures, but derive pleasure from observing their efforts at raiding bird feeders. In Great Britain, a few birders have even taken this enjoyment to a new level. "Daylight Robbery,"a television documentary produced in England, displays the efforts of some backyard naturalists in creating unique and complicated obstacle courses for squirrels. In order to reach the supply of food, the squirrels are challenged by a series of complex mechanisms and gadgets. As each new barrier is thwarted, new complexities are added. The result is the beginning of a new urban wildlife activity: competitive squirrel-proofing.

SQUIRREL HOUSES

"The beauty and delicacy of this animal induced me to attempt taming and domesticating some of them, but without success; for though several of them were so familiar as to take any thing out of my hand, and sit on the table where I was writing, and play with the pens, &c. yet they never would bear to be handled, and were very mischievous; gnawing the chair-bottoms, window-curtains, sashes, &c. to pieces." — Samuel Hearne

Squirrels in the wild have little problem finding suitable nesting sites. However, in urban and suburban locations, a lack of trees and competition for space with other squirrels often drives these animals to move into structures built for humans. Once established, a squirrel nesting habit may be hard to break, leaving the human occupants of a structure with unwanted noise, parasites, smell, and damage to wiring, woodwork, and insulation.

Custom squirrel houses may help reduce this risk, and promote healthier urban squirrel populations, not to mention improved human-squirrel relations. Squirrel houses are no more complicated than bird houses, requiring only minor scraps of wood and proper placement to attract occupants.

Placement of squirrel houses.

1. Hang in trees or on poles or away from buildings.

2. Height above ground: at least 15 feet (3 meters).

3. Locate away from the prevailing wind.

4. Face to south, into the sun.

5. Open box to clean in mid-to-late summer. Don't disturb if there are babies present.

DO-IT-YOURSELF SQUIRREL HOUSE

**USE UNFINISHED CEDAR,
FIR, OR REDWOOD**

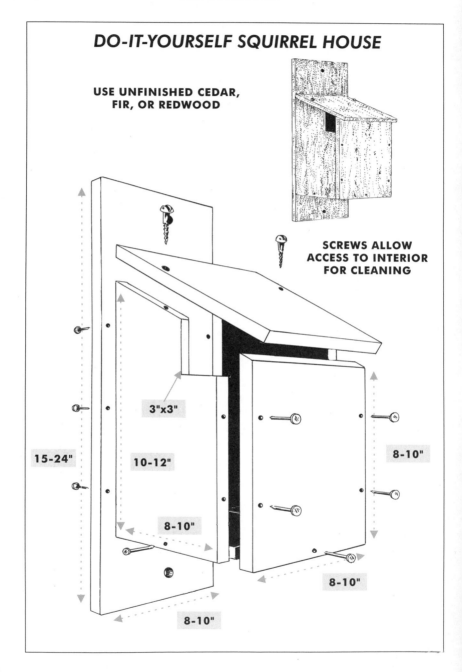

**SCREWS ALLOW
ACCESS TO INTERIOR
FOR CLEANING**

3"x3"

15-24"

10-12"

8-10"

8-10"

8-10"

8-10"

8-10"

SQUIRREL REMOVAL

"Man alive, I'm a telling you
The fiddles and guitars really flew
That Ford took off like a flying squirrel
Flew halfway around the world
Scattered wives and children
All over the side of that mountain."
— Woody Guthrie, "Talking Dust Bowl Blues"

Even squirrel lovers may sometimes have to admit that the squirrel may be a problem animal. And in urban habitats, too many squirrels can make life unpleasant. If squirrels cannot be kept from destroying gardens, wiring, or structures, exile may be an appropriate solution.

Many cities provide such service for residents. Animal control officers use live traps to catch the unwanted critters and transport them to locations where their presence will be less obtrusive. Live traps may also be provided for use by residents on a check-out basis. Some organizations, such as animal shelters and animal humane associations, provide "loaner" live traps to catch and relocate pesky wildlife.

Live traps are very effective for city squirrels. Accustomed to the presence of humans and human contraptions, live traps rarely have to be disguised or hidden in urban conditions. The bait of choice for squirrels: peanut butter.

Successfully trapping squirrels may be easier than finding them new homes. Squirrels — especially gray squirrels, the most common variety in cities — can find their way back to their original neighborhoods unless transported more than a few miles away. Some experienced squirrel movers consider any distance under five miles inadequate.

The most serious problem facing a squirrel when being forcibly relocated is the established presence of other squirrels in their new location. If a squirrel is released in an area where there are existing squirrels, the newcomer will create a disruption because it has not yet been established in the local order of dominance. If the existing squirrels are more aggressive, it will be driven farther away until an unused territory can be found. If the new squirrel is more dominant, one or more of the existing squirrels will suffer the same fate. The consequence may be injuries, stress, and even death.

This situation may be even more deadly to the transported squirrel depending on the weather and season of the year.

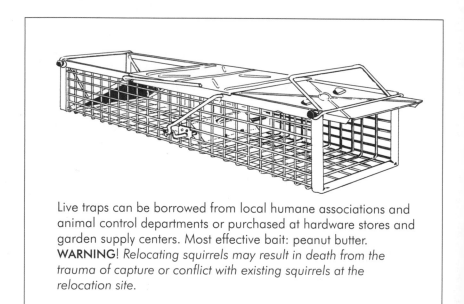

Live traps can be borrowed from local humane associations and animal control departments or purchased at hardware stores and garden supply centers. Most effective bait: peanut butter. **WARNING!** *Relocating squirrels may result in death from the trauma of capture or conflict with existing squirrels at the relocation site.*

ENDANGERED
SQUIRRELS

"Leaving others to their own judgment on this subject, we can say for ourselves that on many occasions when studying the varied characters of the inferior creatures, we have felt that we were reading lessons taught us by nature, that were calculated to make us wiser and better."
— John Audubon, John Bachman, 1840

Squirrels may be a common animal in many parts of the continent, but there are species of squirrels which are endangered. According to the United States Office of Endangered Species, tree squirrels considered rare enough to be on the endangered species list in the United States are:

CAROLINA NORTHERN FLYING SQUIRREL

This subspecies of the northern flying squirrel is found in isolated areas in four states, North Carolina, Tennessee, Virginia, and West Virginia. Its preferred habitat is higher slopes and elevations in the Appalachian Mountains in transition zones between hardwood forests and conifer forests.

VIRGINIA NORTHERN FLYING SQUIRREL

This subspecies of the northern flying squirrel is found in isolated areas in four states, North Carolina, Tennessee, Virginia, and West Virginia. Its preferred habitat is higher slopes and elevations in the Appalachian Mountains in transition zones between hardwood forests and conifer forests.

DELMARVA PENINSULA FOX SQUIRREL

The home range for this animal was originally Delaware, eastern Maryland, southeastern Pennsylvania, and part of the Delmarva Peninsula. The Delmarva Peninsula extends south from Wilmington, Delaware, with Delaware Bay and the Atlantic Ocean on the east and the Chesapeake Bay on the west. The Peninsula includes parts of Delaware, Maryland, and Virginia.

The remaining population is confined to this Peninsula, primarily in four counties in Maryland and the Chincoteague National Wildlife Refuge in Accomac County, Virginia. This fox squirrel's preferred habitat is mature hardwood forest and groves of conifers.

MOUNT GRAHAM RED SQUIRREL

It now exists only in southeastern Arizona on the slopes of the Pinaleño Mountains, primarily on Mount Graham. The Mount Graham squirrels live at elevations from 7,800 feet to 10,720 feet.

These animals have all fallen victim to the spread of civilization. Expanding cities, the transformation of forests into farm fields and pastures, and logging have reduced their natural habitats, and their populations have gradually shrunk in size. Each of these subspecies is adapted to a specific habitat, limiting its ability to find new territory as its preferred habitat shrinks.

Over time, protection and reintroduction efforts on the part of wildlife groups may give them a second chance, but the odds are not in their favor. A single forest fire, for example, could reduce the remaining population of Mount Graham red squirrels to a non-sustaining point, turning their current endangered condition into certain doom.

Illustration by Thomas Bewick (1824, *The Figures of Bewick's Quadrapeds*)

PROFILE OF A SQUIRREL

The Mount Graham red squirrel was added to the federal endangered species list on June 3, 1987. This squirrel species has existed as an isolated colony since the advance and retreat of the glaciers in the Pleistocene era, from 1.8 million to 10,000 years ago. It now exists only in southeastern Arizona on the slopes of the Pinaleño Mountains, primarily on Mount Graham. The Mount Graham squirrels live at elevations of from 7,800 feet to 10,720 feet. Their habitat of choice is the spruce and fir forest native to the highest elevations with some squirrels also living in mixed conifer forests farther down the slopes. The population is estimated to be about 1000 animals, although annual fluctuations related to the natural production of pine cones may double this number or reduce it by half. Further reductions are also likely from construction activity on Mount Graham. In the 1990s, the University of Arizona is building a new astronomical observatory near the peak, removing the choicest habitat of the red squirrel in the process.

VITAL STATISTICS Color grayish brown with reddish or rust-colored tinge on back, lighter belly, dark line separates back color from belly. Ears tufted in winter. Smaller than other red squirrels.

LENGTH Body 8 inches (20 cm); tail 5 inches (14 cm).

PREFERRED TREES Englemann spruce, corkbark fir. Also Douglas fir, white fir.

THREAT FACTORS Logging has been the chief enemy of this squirrel. Intensive logging in the region since early in the century has reduced the preferred native habitat, mature conifer forests at high elevations.

PARASITES

*"Quadrapeds and birds have certain antipathies:
they are capable of experiencing many of the feelings
that appertain to mankind; they are susceptible of
passion, are sometimes spiteful and revengeful, and are
wise enough to know their "natural enemies" without a
formal introduction."* — John James Audubon, John Bachman

Like most mammals, squirrels are an object of attraction for many parasites. Organisms such as ticks, fleas, mites, lice, flies, chiggers, tapeworms, threadworms, and protozoa pester these animals and can lead to disease and occasionally, death.

Diseases affecting tree squirrel populations include California encephalitis virus; western equine encephalitis; plague; leptospirosis; tularemia; tetanus; leporipoxviruses, Silverwater virus, Powassan virus, ringworm, and mange.

Flying squirrels are also known to be a host to typhus (spread by lice) — the same form that has been a menace to humans — although few human cases have been reported to be caused by contact with these squirrels. With few exceptions, diseases affect only isolated squirrels; epidemics of any kind are rare. Rabies, one of the few diseases of wild animals that is a persistent and serious threat to humans, is also rarely reported in squirrels. Humans bitten or scratched by squirrels are mostly threatened with localized infections, and in isolated incidents, tetanus.

Two parasites cause visible problems for American tree squirrels. One, the *mange mite*, is a specialized mite which burrows into the skin of squirrels and lays its eggs. After hatching, the larvae crawl around on the surface of the skin and burrow into hair follicles as they change into nymphs. Large infestations of these insects cause patches of hair to fall out, resulting in a distinctive "mangy" looking squirrel. Infestations also often cause secondary infections. If this coincides with conditions of low food availability, over-crowding, or severe weather, squirrels can die from the effects.

Another insect causing visible effects on squirrels is the *bot fly*, also known as the *warble fly*. Bot flies of the genus *Cuterebra* have evolved to target tree squirrels. The adult flies lay their eggs in or near squirrel nests; after hatching, bot fly larvae seek out and burrow into the skin of the squirrels. Inside the skin, the larvae create their own nests, forming cysts and getting oxygen by piercing through the skin of the squirrel with breathing tubes. The result is often a conspicuous swelling on the body of a squirrel. Hunters have traditionally abandoned such squirrels if a bot fly cyst is present, although the squirrel is otherwise unspoiled. When left alone, the larvae eventually leaves the squirrel — usually during the fall months — to pursue the next stage in its development. Bot fly infestations are thought to vary between 7 and 50 percent in squirrel populations.

The northern flying squirrel is susceptible to a parasite, the nematode *Strongyloides*, one of several specialized

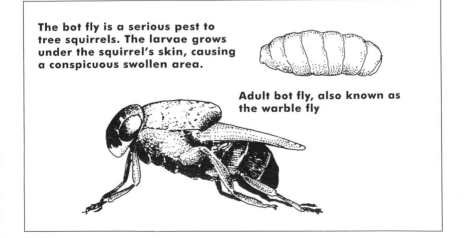

The bot fly is a serious pest to tree squirrels. The larvae grows under the squirrel's skin, causing a conspicuous swollen area.

Adult bot fly, also known as the warble fly

worms that infect animals. In parts of its southernmost range this parasite may be reducing or eliminating squirrels in this species, particularly two of the endangered squirrel species, the Virginia northern flying squirrel and the Carolina northern flying squirrel. The southern flying squirrel, on the other hand, is thought to be immune to the effects of this pest and members of that species may gradually be taking over territory lost to its northern counterpart because of its effect.

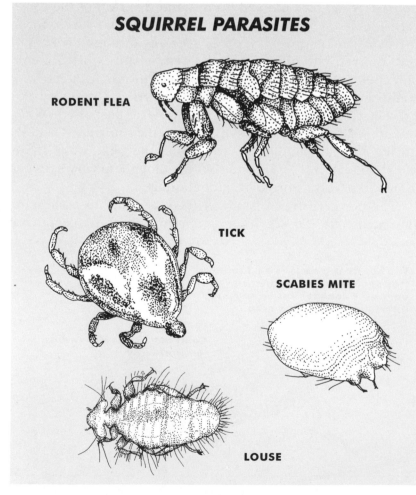

SQUIRREL PARASITES

RODENT FLEA

TICK

SCABIES MITE

LOUSE

CAUSES OF DEATH

"The squirrel that you kill in jest dies in earnest."

— Henry David Thoreau

Squirrels, like most small mammals, do not normally live more than a few years in the wild. Most tree squirrels may survive for up to four or five years, but only in captivity are longer life spans common.

In previous eras, when squirrels were a prime source of food and most of the human population lived in rural areas, trapping and hunting was a major source of mortality. The number of tree squirrels killed by hunters even in recent years may be in the millions, but the squirrel population is not thought to be seriously affected because of its ability to rebound.

In modern times, in any case, a general decline in hunting and trapping has reduced these activities as a threat to most animals in North America. Humans, however, continue to exert a deadly toll on squirrels, and now it may be the automobile as well as the rifle or shotgun that is the weapon. In cities, suburbs, parks, and forests, the proximity of traffic may result in more squirrel deaths than any other cause except disease and starvation. Some biologists may even use the number of "road kill" squirrels to monitor the size of a local squirrel population; the more squirrels hit by cars, the higher the local population.

The greatest cause of death for squirrels is a combination punch: lack of food, the presence of secondary infections from diseases (particularly those related to damage from the mange mite), and the effects of severe cold weather. This three-part threat is thought to account for the greatest number of deaths.

SQUIRREL PREDATORS

MINK

FISHER

WILDCAT

RED FOX

COYOTE

Weather incidents can also be deadly. High winds, extreme cold, ice storms, high water, and other side effects of the climate can be hard on squirrels. This is especially true for young squirrels while still in the nest, when wind storms are a threat to survival. Older squirrels are generally not threatened by severe weather unless they are weakened by disease or scarcity of food.

In urban areas, squirrels may be preyed upon more by domestic animals than their traditional enemies. Cats and dogs are a threat to young squirrels in backyards and parks, but adult squirrels are usually capable of detecting and avoiding these threats.

During periods of movement from one area to another, squirrels may drown while crossing bodies of water. Although they are natural swimmers, fatigue and rough water conditions can be too much for their abilities. Reports from historical records and more contemporary observations indicate that while swimming, squirrels may also become food for aquatic predators. Large fish such as bass, lake trout, muskellunge, northern pike, gar, and others have been seen attacking swimming squirrels, and squirrel bodies have been found in the stomach contents of these type of fish. Other water-dwelling threats that occasionally feast on squirrels include snapping turtles, alligators, and pelicans.

Encounters with man-made contrivances can be deadly for squirrels. Electrical transmission lines, transformers, and switches are a major source of deadly force, killing thousands of squirrels each year. But even old-fashioned technology can be a threat for some squirrels. Squirrels are noted as frequent visitors to the collection buckets used to gather maple sap in the New England states. Flying squirrels are small enough to occasionally get in trouble at these sites, falling into the sticky liquid and drowning.

Squirrels may also fall victim to their own gymnastic abilities. Falls from trees, telephone lines, bird feeders, and roofs are not uncommon. Injuries and death can result from these falls, although the light weight of the average squirrel and their ability to land on their feet can keep such mishaps from being certain disasters.

A primary threat to squirrels may come from their own species. Squirrels are frequent raiders of their neighbors' nests, and infanticide is one potential outcome. Mother squirrels actively defend their territories and nesting areas, but

MORE SQUIRREL PREDATORS

RED-SHOULDERED HAWK

GOSHAWK

GREAT HORNED OWL

EASTERN DIAMONDBACK

may be distracted or be away from the nest while feeding. Both male and female squirrels are known to kill infants. Other raiders of nests include the raccoon, which some biologists believe may be the major predator of young squirrels, tree-climbing snakes, martens, weasels, and other climbing carnivores.

Natural predators of squirrels are now scarce in some parts of the country. Even where prevalent, tree squirrels are not thought to be the predominate part of any predator's diet. Depending on the animal and the availability of squirrels, this would mean no more than 1-10 percent of the predator's diet. Among carnivores, the pine marten is considered to be the deadliest threat to tree squirrels.

The most consistent threat from predators for squirrels is from the air. Raptors, both during the day and the night, target squirrels as a favorite food source. Because of the large size of gray and fox squirrels, however, adults face a problem only from the larger birds such as the great horned owl (usually only a problem for squirrels active after nightfall), large hawks, and eagles. Small squirrels — red squirrels, flying squirrels, and juvenile squirrels — may attract smaller raptors and even crows or ravens.

In general, adult squirrels are less threatened than their young by predators. When in the nest or just emerging into the world, young squirrels are frequently attacked by tree-climbing snakes, ground snakes, raccoons, opossums, foxes, coyotes, and bobcats. On some occasions, usually triggered by stress because of over-crowding or lack of food, adult squirrels will attack babies or juveniles. Some biologists have also reported incidents of mother squirrels eating their own babies, most likely because they are ill or deformed.

Among the squirrels, the smallest species — northern and southern flying squirrels — are most often the target of predators. The fox squirrel, the largest North American tree squirrel, has the least to fear. In urban and suburban areas, house cats may be the most consistent threat to squirrels, particularly to juveniles just out of the nest.

Squirrels usually experience the greatest loss of life during the first year of life. An estimated 15-25 percent of young squirrels are thought to survive to the end of their first year. After the first year, squirrels survive at the rate of 50-70 percent per year. About 1 percent of the squirrels born in a given year will live longer than 5 years.

Squirrels can live for as long as a decade but predators and disease are likely to kill them before this. In captivity tree squirrels have lived as long as twenty years, at least this was the lifespan of one zoo-dwelling gray squirrel. Squirrels in zoos in the United States and Europe have been common since the 1800s, when emerging interest in natural history prompted many cities, scientific societies, and individual collectors to use caged animals to study animal behavior, evolution (first referred to as the "transmutation" of species), and taxonomy.

Reports from zoos about squirrels show a range of lifespans of up to 11 years for a western gray squirrel. One southern flying squirrel lived for more than 7 years; an eastern gray squirrel was at least 8 years old; a fox squirrel was reported to live for 13 years; and more than one red squirrel survived beyond 9 years.

PINE MARTEN
(Martes americana)

PROFILE OF A PREDATOR

*"They are agile and graceful in their movements; and, if
not really more active than the Weasels, their actions
seem to possess a quality of lightness and elasticity ...
An expert climber, quite at home in the leafy intricacies of
tree tops, it pursues Squirrels, and goes birds'-nesting with
success."* — Elliott Coue

One of the most specialized carnivores in North America
is the pine marten (*Martes americana*), also known as
the American sable. Similar to the mink and the fisher, the
marten is a low, sleek animal about half the size of a house
cat, from 20-30 inches in length, weighing from 1 to 4
pounds. The marten's traditional range is throughout Canada,
Alaska, the northwestern states, the Rocky Mountain region,
and east through the Great Lake states and New England. Its
preferred habitat is conifer forests.

In the past few centuries the marten was extensively
trapped for its fur, reducing its population and removing it
entirely from part of its original range. In recent decades,
however, it has gradually began to rebound in numbers.

Martens are a formidable threat to squirrels because of their
agility and speed in the trees. They are capable of chasing and
catching most squirrels because of their ability to rapidly
climb trunks and limbs and their athletic leaps from tree to
tree. In Europe, martens are also common, and make squirrels
a primary part of their diet. In North America, it is more usual
for martens to have a varied diet, including plants, nuts, eggs,
birds, carrion, honey, other rodents, and small mammals.

EDIBLE SQUIRRELS

*"Many of the inhabitants of our Eastern States refuse to
eat Squirrels of any kind, from some prejudice or other;
but we can assure our readers that the flesh of this
species, and many others, is both tender and
well-flavoured, and when nicely broiled, does
not require a hunter's appetite to recommend it."*

— John Bachman

Although in modern times not a major food source for
humans, squirrels were traditionally part of the diet for
both native Americans and immigrants. Squirrel variations
included baked, stuffed, pie, stew, fried, roast, soup, pilau,
broiled, and grilled. During food shortages in Europe in
World War II, the Vicomte de Mauduit recommended squirrel
and rooks as meat alternatives: "Squirrel is also most tasty
roasted." (1940, *They Can't Ration These*).

Audubon remarked that the "cat" squirrel (fox squirrel)
was considered of "superior quality" for eating. In his jour-
neys to research his book on the mammals of North America
(*The Viviparous Quadrupeds of North America*) he remarked
that they were being sold for 37 1/2 cents in the markets of
New York City, while gray squirrels were being sold for only
12 1/2 cents.

Squirrel hunting has declined in popularity in the twentieth
century, not because there are fewer squirrels, but because of
the general trend away from hunting. Much of this decline
has come because fewer people live in rural areas with close
proximity to game. At the same time, the culture of the
continent has focused new attention on the value of wildlife
and the preservation of wild flora and fauna.

Traditionally, squirrels have been an elusive target for hunters. Their natural instincts and abilities keep them alert for potential danger, including humans, and allow them maximum capability for camouflage and evasion. Finding and shooting a squirrel in the fall or winter when bare branches minimize potential hiding places is hard enough; in the summer months when leafy canopies provide dense cover, squirrels elude all but the most skilled hunters.

Because of the small size of a squirrel, hunting has traditionally been pursued with small caliber rifles or shotguns. Canny frontiersmen typically attempted to avoid wasting meat by destroying it with bullets. The best method for bagging this game — although only the best marksmen could achieve success — was "barking," aiming at the bark under or next to a squirrel. The intention was to stun the squirrel with the impact, knocking it from the tree without actually hitting it with a shot. Although this method is widely reported in historical records, some experts believe it to be mostly a myth, an exaggeration of hunting skill.

Squirrels are notoriously difficult targets. Finding these aboreal mammals is the hardest part of the hunt because of the normal instinct of tree squirrels when evading danger from below. They stretch out on the top of branches, flattened against the bark. The result is a minimalized profile and the maximum camouflage effect from the natural colors of their fur. When fleeing up the trunks of trees, squirrels also instinctively run around the trunk, putting the tree between themselves and the vision of their pursuers. An individual walking around the tree is unlikely to see this animal as it continuously adjusts its position, keeping to the opposite side.

Hunters may counter this behavior by hunting in pairs or using a dog to flush the squirrel back into the line of sight. Raptors often do this instinctively when hunting squirrels, pairs of hawks working in tandem to break down the defense.

Squirrels in excessive numbers once prompted massive action through hunting. So many squirrels existed in many eastern states in the 1700s that agricultural crops were threatened, a serious problem in an era when crop failures might mean starvation. One result was bounties placed on squirrels. In 1749, such a bounty was imposed by the state of Pennsylvania, an offer of threepence (three cents) for each dead squirrel. This resulted in so many demands for payment that the state was forced to repeal the bounty in order to forestall bankruptcy.

Local squirrel hunting contests were common throughout the 1700s and 1800s in many states. By the mid 1800s, however, the razing of forests for crops and pastures and the continuing hunting pressure made squirrel populations less plentiful through much of the east and midwest. Fox squirrels are now absent from New England — the local populations destroyed a century ago — a legacy of this activity.

> *"Wilt thou hunt? Kill no more squirrels than you want for your pie, nor more partridges than you want for your spit. To slay these little innocents for mere sport is a waste of time, money, and morals; your boys had better be collecting materials for making manure, which will make your farm rich, and stop the cry of 'short crops, small potatoes, and hard times.'"*
> — *The Old Farmer's Almanac, 1817*

RESOURCES

Organizations that deal with animal and wildlife issues can provide additional information about squirrels, as well as being useful in local, regional, or national efforts to protect natural habitats and endangered species.

American Humane Association
63 Inverness Drive East
Englewood, CO 80112
303-792-9900

American Society for the Prevention of Cruelty to Animals
424 E. 92nd Street
New York, NY 10128
212-876-7700

Associated Humane Societies
124 Evergreen Avenue
Newark, NJ 07114
201-824-7080

Friends of the Earth
1025 Vermont Avenue NW 3rd Floor
Washington, DC 20005
202-783-7400

Humane Society of the United States
2100 L Street NW
Washington, DC 20037
202-452-1100

International Wildlife Rehabilitation Council
4437 Central Place Suite B-4
Suison, CA 94585
707-864-1761

National Audubon Society
700 Broadway
New York, NY 10003
212-979-3000

National Wildlife Federation
1400 16th Street NW
Washington, DC 20036-2266
202-797-6800

National Wildlife Health Foundation
c/o James L. Naviaux
606 El Pintado Road
Danville, CA 94526
510-939-3456

National Wildlife Rehabilatators Association
14 North 7th Avenue
St. Cloud, MN 56303
612-259-4086

The Nature Conservancy
1815 N. Lynn Street
Arlington, VA 22209
703-841-5300

Wilderness Society
900 17th Street NW
Washington, DC 20006-2596
202-833-2300

Wildlife Preservation Trust International
3400 West Girad Avenue
Philadelphia, PA 19104
215-222-3636

Wildlife Society
5410 Grosvenor Lane
Bethesda, MD 20814-2197
301-897-9770

ONLINE RESOURCES

Computer connections to information can prove useful to those interested in wildlife and nature. Online resources include reference material, discussions with like-minded individuals, communications with agencies and organizations involved with wildlife, and access to up-to-date information and schedules. As the online industry is growing and evolving rapidly, listed resources may change and new resource may pop up unexpectedly. To search for additional resources, look for menu listings or search for topics associated with **wildlife**, **wild animals**, **nature**, **ecology**, and **environmental resources**. Also look for topics listed by the common name of an animal, such as **squirrel**.

Many libraries now provide access to their materials through online connections. Using terminals inside libraries — or dialing in from a remote location — use the same search strategies to locate books, reference material, and periodicals.

AMERICA ONLINE
Go to <Nature Conservancy> or <Network Earth Online>

COMPUSERVE
Go to <Earth Forum>, <The Great Outdoors Forum>, <Outdoor Network>, or <Animal Forum: Wildlife/Rehab>

WORLD WIDE WEB
Environmental Communicator <www.nwf.org/nwf/home.html>
National Audubon Society <www.audubon.org/audubon>
Sierra Club <www.sierraclub.org>
U.S. Fish & Wildlife Service <www.fws.gov>
The Wildlife Society <www.us.net/wildlife>
Watchable Wildlife <www.gorp.com/wildlife/wwhome.htm>

SQUIRREL AID

Most major cities in North America are home to at least one wild animal rehabilitation center. These organizations, usually associated with a national group such as the *National Wildlife Rehabilitators Association* or the *International Wildlife Rehabilitation Council*, are licensed sites that are qualified to handle and treat injured animals. Squirrels that have been orphaned, attacked by cats, or hit by cars may qualify to be cared for at such centers.

Check local telephone directories or directory assistance to connect with a center if necessary to deal with an injured squirrel. Other options include local chapters of the Dumb Friends League, animal humane societies, veterinarians, and municipal animal shelters.

International Wildlife Rehabilitation Council (IWRC)
4437 Central Place Suite B-4
Suisun, CA 94585

National Wildlife Rehabilitators Association (NWRA)
14 N. 7th Avenue
St. Cloud, MN 56303

Each state has a department of wildlife that can offer advice, guidelines, regulations, and other information about squirrels. These listings can be found in local telephone directories. Appropriate departments or divisions may include: **Wildlife, Fish and Game, Conservation, Natural Resources**, or **Parks**.

SQUIRREL PRODUCTS

Recent public interest in feeding birds has helped expand the availability of retail outlets selling bird feeders and bird food, as well as feeders and food for squirrels. National franchises in this industry have outlets in many major cities.

Petsmart Inc.
10000 N. 31st Avenue
Phoenix, AZ 85085
602-944-7070

Wild Bird Center
5339 Sunrise Boulevard
Fair Oaks, CA 95628
916-966-5958

Wild Birds Unlimited
3003 E. 96th Street
Indianapolis, IN 46240
317-571-7100

The following companies offer a range of products for those interested in attracting, feeding, and housing squirrels.

Arundale Products (squirrel baffles for bird feeders)
P.O. Box 4637
St. Louis, MO 63108

The Birding Company (squirrel baffles for bird feeders)
Woodcrafters Kits Inc.
Yarmouth, ME 04096

Duncraft (squirrel-proof bird feeders)
Penacook, NH 03303-9020

Erva (squirrel baffles for bird feeders)
1895 N. Milwaukee
Chicago, IL 60647

Forest Edge Wildlife Products (squirrel feeders)
3320 Crain Highway
Waldorf, MD 20603

Heath Manufacturing Company (squirrel feeders, baffles)
140 Mill Street
Coopersville, MI 49404-0105

Heritage Farms Division (squirrel-proof bird feeders)
Century Tool & Manufacturing Company
1462 U.S. Route 20 Bypass
P.O. Box 188
Cherry Valley, IL 61016

Homestead Products Inc. (squirrel-proof bird feeders)
17055 W. Victor Road
New Berlin, WI 53151

Kfeeder (squirrel baffles for bird feeders)
4635 Post Road
Warwick, RI 02886

Metz Farms (squirrel feeders)
1650 Broadway NW
Grand Rapids, MI 49504

The Nuttery (squirrel-proof bird feeders)
Dene Road
Northwood, Middlesex
Great Britain HA62DA

Perky Pet (squirrel feeders)
2201 S. Wabash Street
Denver, CO 80231

Wildwood Farms Inc. (squirrel feeders, squirrel food)
P.O. Box 938
Clinton, IA 52733

BIBLIOGRAPHY

Armstrong, David M. *Rocky Mountain Mammals*. 1975, Rocky Mountain Nature Association.

Audubon, John James, and Bachman, John. *The Quadrapeds of North America*. 1851, 1854, V.G. Audubon (New York City).

Ball, Katherine M. *Decorative Motives of Oriental Art*. 1927, Dodd, Mead and Company.

Banfield, A.W.F. *The Mammals of Canada*. 1974, University of Toronto Press.

Barkalow, Frederick S. and Shorten, Monica. *The World of the Grey Squirrel*. 1973, J.B. Lippincott Company.

Benyus, Janine M. *The Field Guide to Wildlife Habitats of the Western United States*. 1989, Fireside/Simon & Schuster.

Bourlière, François. *The Natural History of Mammals*. 1954, Alfred A. Knopf.

Burt, William Henry. *A Field Guide to the Mammals: North America North of Mexico* (3rd edition). 1980, Houghton Mifflin Company.

Chapman, Joseph A. and Feldhamer, George A. (eds). *Wild Mammals of North America: Biology, Management, and Economics*. 1982, Johns Hopkins University Press (Baltimore, MD).

Clark, Joseph D. *Beastly Folklore*. 1968, Scarecrow Press Inc. (Methuchen, NJ).

Coues, Elliott. *Fur-Bearing Mammals*. 1877, Government Printing Office. Republished: 1970, Arno Press.

Crandall, Lee S. *Management of Wild Mammals in Captivity*. 1964, University of Chicago Press.

Curtis, Edward S. *The North American Indian*. 1928. Republished: 1976, Johnson Reprint Corporation.

Dennis, John V. *The Wildlife Gardener*. 1985, Alfred A. Knopf.

Elton, Charles S. *The Pattern of Animal Communities*. 1966, John Wiley & Sons/Methuen & Company.

Fairbairn, James (comp.). *Fairbairn's Book of Crests of the Families of Great Britain and Ireland* (4th edition). 1892. Republished: 1968, Heraldic Book Company (Baltimore).

Fleharty, Eugene D. *Wild Animals and Settlers on the Great Plains.* 1995, University of Oklahoma Press (Norman, OK).

Friedmann, Herbert. *A Bestiary for Saint Jerome: Animal Symbolism in European Religious Art.* 1980, Smithsonian Institution Press (Washington, DC).

Gambaryan, P.P. *How Mammals Run.* 1974, John Wiley & Sons/Israel Program for Scientific Translation.

George, Wilma. *Animals and Maps.* 1969, Martin Secker and Warburg Limited (London).

Godin, Alfred J. *Wild Mammals of New England.* 1977, Johns Hopkins University Press (Baltimore, MD).

Gotch, A.F. *Mammals: Their Latin Names Explained.* 1979, Blandford Press Ltd. (Dorset, United Kingdom).

Grose, Captain. *1811 Dictionary of the Vulgar Tongue: A Dictionary of Buckish Slang, University Wit, and Pickpocket Eloquence.* 1984, Bibliophile Books (London). Reissue of edition by Captain Grose, 1811, C. Chappel, London. Published initially in 1785 and 1788 as *A Classical Dictionary of the Vulgar Tongue.*

Grzimek, Dr. Bernhard. *Grzimek's Animal Life Encyclopedia.* 1975, Van Nostrand Reinhold Company.

Gurnell, John. *The Natural History of Squirrels.* 1987, Facts on File Publications.

Halfpenny, James. *A Field Guide to Mammal Tracking in Western America.* 1986, Johnson Books.

Hall, E. Raymond, and Kelson, Keith R. *The Mammals of North America.* 1959, The Ronald Press Company (New York City).

Hamilton, W.J. Jr. *American Mammals: Their Lives, Habits, and Economic Relations.* 1939, McGraw-Hill Book Company, Inc.

Hamilton, William J. Jr., and Whitaker, John O. Jr. *Mammals of the Eastern United States* (2nd edition). 1979, Cornell University Press (Ithaca, NY).

Harrison, Kit, and Harrison, George. *America's Favorite Backyard Wildlife.* 1885, Simon & Schuster.

Headstrom, Richard. *A Complete Field Guide to Nests in the United States.* 1970, Ives Washburn, Inc. (New York, NY).

Hearne, Samuel. *A Journey from Prince of Wale's Fort in Hudson's Bay to the Northern Ocean in the years 1769, 1770, 1771, and 1772.* Republished: 1911, The Champlain Society (Toronto).

Hildebrand, Milton, Bramble, Dennis M., Liem, Karel F., Wake, David B. (eds.). *Functional Vertebrate Morphology.* 1985, Belknap Press/Harvard University Press.

Hoffmeister, Donald F. *Mammals of Arizona.* 1986, The University of Arizona Press and the Arizona Game and Fish Department.

Korth, William W. *The Tertiary Record of Rodents in North America.* 1994, Plenum Press.

Leland, Charles. *The Algonquin Legends of New England: Myths and Folklore of the Micmac, Passamaquoddy, and Penobscot Tribes.* 1884, Houghton, Mifflin & Company.

Leopold, Aldo. *A Sand County Almanac.* 1949, Oxford University Press.

Lowe, David W., Mathews, John Rl, Moseley, Charles J. (eds). *The Official World Wildlife Fund Guide to Endangered Species of North America.* 1990, Beacham Publishing Inc. (Washington, D.C.).

MacClintock, Dorcas. *Squirrels of North America.* 1970, Van Nostrand Reinhold Company.

Martin, Alexander C., Zim, Herbert S., and Nelson, Arnold L. *American Wildlife & Plants: A Guide to Wildlife Food Habits.* 1951, Dover Publications, Inc.

Matthiessen, Peter. *Wildlife in America.* 1995, Penguin Books.

Mearns, Edgar Alexander. *Mammals of the Mexican Boundary of the United States.* 1907, Government Printing Office. Republished: 1970, Arno Press.

Menninger, Edwin A. *Edible Nuts of the World.* 1977, Horticultural Books, Inc. (Stuart, Florida).

Merilees, Bill. *Attracting Backyard Wildlife: A Guide for Nature Lovers.* 1989, Voyageur Press (Stillwater, MN).

Meyer, Steve. *Being Kind to Animal Pests: A No-Nonsense Guide to Humane Animal Control with Cage Traps.* 1991, Steve Meyer (Garrison, IA).

Mirov, Nicholas T., and Hasbrouck, Jean. *The Story of Pines.* 1976, Indiana University Press.

Morgan, Lewis H. *League of the Ho-Dé-No-Sau-Nee.* 1901, Burt Franklin (New York, NY).

Nelson, Edward W. *Wild Animals of North America.* 1918, National Geographic Society.

Noyes, John H., and Progulske, Donald R. (eds). *A Symposium on Wildlife in an Urbanizing Environment.* 1973, U.S.D.A. Forest Service, Dept. of Forestry and Wildlife Management (Univ. of Massachusetts), Massachusetts Div. of Fisheries and Game, Massachusetts Cooperative Wildlife Research Unit, Massachsuetts Audubon Society, The Wildlife Society.

Olin, George. *Mammals of the Southwest Mountains and Mesas.* 1961, Southwest Parks and Monuments Association (Globe, AZ).

Peterson, Randolph L. *The Mammals of Eastern Canada.* 1966, Oxford University Press (Toronto).

Preston, Richard J. Jr. *North American Trees.* 1961, Iowa State University Press.

Puckett, Newbell Niles. *Folk Beliefs of the Southern Negro.* 1926, University of North Carolina Press. Republished: 1968, Negro Universities Press/Greenworld Publishing Corp. (New York, NY).

Rosengarten, Frederic Jr. *The Book of Edible Nuts.* 1984, Walker & Company.

Rue, Leonard Lee III. *Sportsman's Guide to Game Animals: A Field Book of North American Species.* 1968, Outdoor Life Books/Harper & Row.

Savage, R.J.G., and Long, M.R. *Mammal Evolution: An Illustrated Guide.* 1986, Facts on File/The British Museum.

Schoolcraft, Henry R. *Narrative Journal of Travels through the Northwestern Regions of the United States Extending from Detroit through the Great Chain of American Lakes to the Sources of the Mississippi River in the Year 1820.* 1855, Philadelphia. Republished: 1953, The Michigan State College Press.

Schwartz, Charles W., and Schwartz, Elizabeth R. *The Wild Mammals of Missouri.* 1981, University of Missouri Press/Missouri Department of Conservation.

Sealander, John A., and Heidt, Gary A. *Arkansas Mammals: Their Natural History, Classification, and Distribution.* 1990, The University of Arkansas Press (Fayetteville, AR).

Seton, Ernest Thompson. *Lives of Game Animals: An Account of Those Land Animals in America, North of the Mexican Border, Which Are Considered "Game," Either Because They Have Held the Attention of Sportsmen, or Received the Protection of Law.* 1928, Doubleday, Doran & Company (Garden City, NY).

Siegel, Ronald K. *Intoxication: Life in Pursuit of Artificial Paradise.* 1989, E.P. Dutton.

Smythe, R.H. *Animal Habits: The Things Animals Do.* 1962, Charles C. Thomas, Publisher (Springfield, IL).

Spencer, Colin, and Clifton, Claire. *The Faber Book of Food.* 1993, Faber and Faber Ltd (London).

Thompson, David. *Explorations in Western America 1784-1812.* Republished: 1916, The Champlain Society (Toronto).

Vander Wall, Stephen B. *Food Hoarding in Animals.* 1990, The University of Chicago Press.

Webster, William David, Parnell, James F., and Biggs, Walter C. Jr. *Mammals of the Carolinas, Virginia, and Maryland.* 1985, The University of North Carolina Press (Chapel Hill, NC).

Weigl, Peter D., Steele, Michael A., Sherman, Lori J., Ha, James C., and Sharpe, Terry L. *The Ecology of the Fox Squirrel (Sciurus Niger) in North Carolina.* 1989, Tall Timbers Research Station (Tallahassee, FL).

Wells-Gosling, Nancy. *Flying Squirrels: Gliders in the Dark.* 1985, Smithsonian Institution Press.

West, George A. *Tobacco Pipes and Smoking Customs of the American Indians.* 1934, Bulletin of the Public Museum of the City of Milwaukee.

Whitaker, John O. Jr. *National Audubon Society Field Guide to North American Mammals.* 1980, Alfred A. Knopf.

Woods, Shirley E. *The Squirrels of Canada.* 1980, National Museums of Canada.

Zeveloff, Samuel I. *Mammals of the Intermountain West.* 1988, University of Utah Press (Salt Lake City).

INDEX

Abert's squirrel 21, 24, 54-57, 73, 87, 98, 120, 123, 126, 133
Abert's squirrel illustration 54
Abert's squirrel range 57
Abert's squirrel vital statistics 55
acorn growth stages 85
Acorn Menu 103
acorns 85, 86, 88, 92, 102-104, 105
Africa 65
African Americans 12
African bush squirrel 64, 65
African giant squirrel 65
age 79, 80
aggression 126, 150
agriculture 2, 16, 97, 134, 136, 152, 166
albino squirrels 74, 77
amanita mushrooms 95
anatomy 68, 68, 71-80
ancestry 67
animal food sources 91
aphrodisiac 65
Arizona gray squirrel 20, 58, 123
Arizona gray squirrel vital statistics 58
Asia 65
Asian mythology 8
Audubon, John James 15, 20, 21, 66, 70, 134, 164
automobiles 157
baby squirrels 127, 128
Bachman, Reverend John 15, 70
baculum 127
balance 79, 114, 160
bark 88, 92, 97, 121, 132, 137
bark stripping 65, 132, 137, 165
beavers 61, 67
beetles 119
berries 97, 105, 112
bibliography 173-178
bird feed 141
bird feeders 92, 140, 142, 143, 144, 171-172
birds' nests 118
biting 138
black magic 12
blue jays 110, 111
bobcats 161
bones 68, 69, 95, 112, 127
bot fly 155
bounties 18, 97, 134, 166

breeding activity 126
caching (see *hoarding*)
camouflage 165
Carolina northern flying squirrel 151, 156
carrion 95, 112
catkins 102
cats 159, 162
chiggers 154
Chinese mythology 8
chipmunks 63, 97
Christian art 8
classification 59
claws 79, 114
climbing 78, 114
colonies, American 16, 18, 97, 164
color detection 72
color phases 22, 74
coloration 76, 77, 79
communication 80
comparing squirrel sizes 24
corn 97, 137, 141, 145
coyotes 158, 161
crossbill finch 88
currency 19
cycles of food production 106
daylight activity 115
Delmarva peninsula fox squirrel 151
dental formula 63
desert ground squirrels 63
diet 81-105
digging 108, 109
disease 122, 154, 157
dogs 159
Do-it-yourself Squirrel Feeder 145
Do-it-yourself Squirrel House 148
dominance 126
Douglas squirrel 21, 24, 42-45, 73, 87, 87, 98, 101, 120, 123, 133
Douglas squirrel illustration 42
Douglas squirrel range 45
Douglas squirrel vital statistics 118
droppings 132
eagles 161
ear tufts 73
ears 72-73
eastern diamondback 160
edible squirrels 164
effigies 7, 11

effigy tobacco pipes 7
eastern gray squirrel 26-29, 87, 120, 123
eastern gray squirrel illustration 26
eastern gray squirrel lifespan 162
eastern gray squirrel range 29
eastern gray squirrel vital statistics 29
electrical power systems 138, 159
endangered squirrels 151-153
England 65, 136, 146
Eocene era 63, 67, 70
estrus 75, 126
European Americans 12
European red squirrel 64, 65, 88, 136
eyes 72
fall reshuffle 136
falls 160
farmland 2, 16, 97
favorite foods 87
feeding behavior 92
feeding birds 140
feeding squirrels 141
feet 78-79, 114, 131
female squirrels 78, 122, 125, 126, 127, 129
fighting 126
fir trees 98
first aid 138
fish 115, 159
fisher 158
fleas 154, 156
flies 154
flying squirrel 15, 24, 63, 65, 72, 79,
   116-117, 119, 120, 122, 128, 130, 131,
   132, 133, 151, 154, 155, 156, 159, 161
folk recipe 12
folklore 12
food debris 130
food trees 89
forest ecosystem 1
fox squirrel 2, 22, 24, 34-37, 70, 87, 110,
   111, 113, 120, 122, 123, 129, 130, 131,
   132, 133, 137, 151, 161, 164, 166
fox squirrel illustration 34
fox squirrel lifespan 162
fox squirrel range 37
fox squirrel vital statistics 35
fruit 141
fungi (see *mushrooms*)
fur 14, 75-78, 163
German mythology 13
gestation periods 127
giant flying squirrel 64
gliding 79

gnawing 59, 71, 92, 95, 121, 132, 137,
   141
good luck charms 13
goshawk 160
grasping 78
gray squirrel 2, 20, 24, 65, 70, 74, 76,
   91, 92, 108, 110, 113, 122, 126, 129,
   132, 133, 134-136, 150, 161, 164
Great Britain (see England)
great horned owl 160
Greek 3, 20, 59
ground squirrels 63
guard hairs 75, 76
hardwood forests 81, 111, 136
hawks 160, 161, 165
head twitching 97
hearing 72-73
heraldry 5
heritage 1
hibernation 115
hiding 165
hoarding 73, 84, 85, 95, 101, 105,
   106-112, 115
Home Turf 123
hopping 113, 114
hummingbird feeders 146
hunting 16, 18, 19, 157, 164, 165, 166
incisors 62, 67, 71
Indian giant squirrel 65
infanticide 160, 161
injuries 160
insects 95, 154, 155
intoxication 97
Ireland 1
iron industry 1
jaw strength 87
juveniles 161, 162
kaibab squirrel 22
kangaroo rats 61
lanes of travel 114
larder hoarding 107, 108, 111
Latin 3, 20, 21, 22, 59
leaf nests 118
legends 6
lice 154, 156
lifespan 157, 162
litter size 125, 128
litters 125, 127, 128
live traps 149, 150
lodgepole pine 101
mammals 60, 62
mange mite 122, 154, 155, 157

maple sugar 95, 159
marksmanship 19, 165
marmots 63
martens 161, 162, 163
mass movement 134-136, 159
mast years 81, 84, 102, 106
mating 126, 127
measurements 25
meat 95
melanism 77
middens 101, 107, 109
Middle Ages 1
migration (see *mass movements*)
milk 128
minerals 95
Miocene era 63, 67
misidentification 16, 66, 70, 77
mite 154, 156
molars 71
molting 75
mortality 157, 162
moth balls 139
mothering 128, 160
Mount Graham red squirrel 152, 153
mountain beavers 61
movement 113-115, 159
mushrooms 93, 95, 96, 105, 107, 112
myths 6, 8, 12, 14, 129, 165
names 2, 3, 4, 13, 17, 19
native Americans 1, 7, 9, 10, 11, 18, 97, 164
natural cooperation 96
nest cavities 121
nest varieties 120
nestling birds 91, 95
nests 118-121, 122, 147, 160, 161
Norse mythology 8
northern flying squirrel 20, 24, 50-53, 87, 95, 116, 117, 123, 151, 155, 161
northern flying squirrel illustration 50
northern flying squirrel range 53
northern flying squirrel vital statistics 51
notching 92, 112
nursing 128
Nut Menu 82
Nut Tree Cycles 84
nut trees 89
nuts 15, 73, 74, 81, 82, 83, 88, 92, 110, 112, 122, 130, 136, 137
oak trees 86, 88, 92, 95, 102-104
obstacle courses 146
oil glands 74
Olney, Illinois 74

omens 13
online resources 169
Orange-bellied squirrel 66
Oriental tree squirrels 65
oxidation 101
paramyids 67, 70
parasites 119, 122, 154-156
patagium 116
penis 127
pest behavior 137, 140, 149
pigment 77
pine cone cross-section 99
pine cone cycles 84
Pine Cone Menu 90
pine cone parts 100
pine cones 85, 86, 88, 90, 92, 98-101, 100, 101, 105, 107, 108, 109, 111, 112, 137
pine forests 163
pine marten 161, 162, 163
pine nuts 99
pine trees 85, 86, 89, 90, 96, 98, 99, 100, 101
pipes 7
plant food sources 94
pocket gophers 61
population cycles 125
population densities 1, 123, 124, 134, 139, 166
postage stamps 19
prairie dogs 63
predators 72, 80, 133, 158, 160, 161, 163
Profile of a Predator 163
Profile of a Squirrel 153
pygmy squirrel 65
rabies 139, 154
raccoon 161
raptors 160, 161, 165
red squirrel 20, 24, 38-41, 65, 76, 84, 85, 87, 95, 98, 101, 106, 108, 111, 113, 120, 122, 123, 127, 129, 132, 133, 152, 153
red squirrel illustration 38
red squirrel lifespan 162
red squirrel range 41
red squirrel vital statistics 39
red-shouldered hawk 160
removal 149-150
repellent 139
reproduction 75, 125-129
resources 167-172

rodents 59, 60, 62, 67, 71
running 113, 114
sap 92, 159
scabies 156
scaly-tailed squirrels 61
scat 132
scatter hoarding 107, 108, 109
scent marking 73
scrotum 129
seasonal diet 105
seasons 111, 112, 115, 134, 136
seedlings 86
seeds 94
serotinous pine cone 85, 86, 101
sessile cones 101
shrubs 89, 97, 138
signs 133
sizes 24
skeleton 68
skull 69
smell 73, 92, 96, 110, 115, 126
snakes 160, 161
snapping turtles 159
soaring 116, 117
softwood trees 81
sounds 133
southern flying squirrel 20, 24, 46-49, 87,
    110, 111, 116, 117, 123, 156, 161
southern flying squirrel illustration 46
southern flying squirrel lifespan 162
southern flying squirrel range 49
southern flying squirrel vital statistics 47
specialized hair 77
species 16, 23, 60
springhares 61
squirrel aid 170
squirrel ancestry 63
squirrel control 18
squirrel family 70
squirrel feeder 145, 171-172
squirrel houses 147, 148
squirrel meat 164
squirrel menace 137-139
squirrel products 171-172
squirrel-proof bird feeders 141, 142, 143,
    171-172
squirrels in motion 113-115
squirreltails 19
stamps 19
starvation 112, 157
stealing 110, 111
suborder 61

sun squirrels 65
superstition 12, 13
sweat glands 74, 78
swimming 115, 159
tactile hairs 77,78
tails 25, 63, 79-80
tapeworms 154
tassel-eared squirrel (see Abert's
    squirrel)
taxonomy 59
teats 129
teeth 25, 59, 62, 63, 71, 92, 138
territory 122-124, 126, 133, 150, 160
testicles 129
tetanus 154
threadworms 154
ticks 154, 156
toes 78
tracks 131
tree anatomy 88
tree squirrels 61, 63
trivia 15, 16, 17
truffles 95
turtle shells 95
turtles 95, 159
underhair 75
urban squirrel survival 139, 141
urban threats 159
urbanization 2, 152
urine 65, 74
vagina 127
vestigial thumb 78
vibrissae 76, 77
Virginia northern flying squirrel 151, 156
volplaning 116
warble fly 155
weather 14, 157, 159
west African sun squirrel 64
western gray squirrel 21, 30-33, 87, 120, 123
western gray squirrel illustration 30
western gray squirrel lifespan 162
western gray squirrel range 33
whiskers 76, 77
wildcat 158
wildlife organizations 167-168, 170
wildlife rehabilitation 170
Woolly flying squirrel 65
World Mammals 60
World Squirrels 64
zoos 162

Other Titles of Interest from Johnson Books

A Field Guide to Mammal Tracking in North America
James Halfpenny

Winter: An Ecological Handbook
James Halfpenny and Roy Ozanne

Soul Among Lions: The Cougar as Peaceful Adversary
Harley Shaw

From Grassland to Glacier:
The Natural History of Colorado and the Surrounding Region
Revised Edition
Cornelia Fleischer Mutel and John C. Emerick

Island in the Plains: A Black Hills Natural History
Edward Raventon

Pocket Nature Guides

Millie Miller and Cyndi Nelson

Hummers: Hummingbirds of North America
Talons: North American Birds of Prey
Early Bird: Western Backyard Birds
Early Bird: Eastern Backyard Birds
Painted Ladies: Butterflies of North America
Chanterelle: A Rocky Mountain Mushroom Book
Kinnikinnick: Rocky Mountain Flowers
Sierra: Sierra Mountain Flowers